KitchenAid®

Baking Companion

WEST
SIDE
PUBLISHING

Special thanks to the staff of KitchenAid.

www.KitchenAid.com

Photography on pages 13, 15, 17, 39, 41, 73, 135, 137, 165, 167, 193, 197, 221, 223 and 225 by Stephen Hamilton Photographics, Inc.

Pictured on the front cover: Individual English Trifles *(page 134)*.
Pictured on the back cover (left to right): Key Lime Bars *(page 12)*, Parmesan Peppercorn Biscuits *(page 220)* and Velvety Coconut and Spice Cake *(page 72)*.

ISBN 13: 978-1-4127-2948-2
ISBN 10: 1-4127-2948-3
UPC: 0-42799-72948-9

Manufactured in China.

8 7 6 5 4 3 2 1

Microwave Cooking: Microwave ovens vary in wattage. Use the cooking times as guidelines and check for doneness before adding more time.

Contents

Glossary of Baking Terms

Beat

Beat: Beating is the technique of stirring or mixing vigorously. Beating introduces air into egg whites, egg yolks, and whipping cream; mixes two or more ingredients to form a homogeneous mixture; or makes a mixture smoother, lighter, and creamier. Beating can be done with a variety of tools, including a spoon, fork, wire whisk, rotary eggbeater, or electric mixer.

Blanch: Blanching means cooking foods, most often vegetables, briefly in boiling water and then quickly cooling them in cold water. Food is blanched for one or more of the following reasons: to loosen and remove skin (tomatoes, peaches, almonds); to enhance color and reduce bitterness (raw vegetables for crudités); and to extend storage life (raw vegetables to be frozen).

Blend: Blending is the technique of mixing together two or more ingredients until they are thoroughly combined. The ingredients may

A GUIDE TO BAKED GOODS

DACQUOISE

A Dacquoise is a classic French cake made of baked nut meringues layered with buttercream filling.

GALETTE

Galette is a French term for a flat round cake. Galettes can be sweet or savory and can be made with puff pastry, sweet pastry, or yeast dough as a base. Popular toppings include fruits, nuts, jams, meats, and cheeses.

GANACHE

Ganache is a rich and decadent chocolate mixture made from semisweet chocolate and boiling cream. Depending upon the proportions of chocolate and cream, ganache can either be used as a cake glaze, a filling, or the base for chocolate confections such as truffles.

MERINGUE

Meringue is a foam made from beating together egg whites and sugar. It can be used as a pie topping or to lighten other mixtures. Simple meringue is be blended together with an electric mixer or electric blender or by hand, using a wooden spoon or wire whisk.

Boil: To bring to a boil means to heat a liquid until bubbles break the surface. Boiling refers to cooking food in boiling water. For a "full rolling boil," bubbles break the surface continuously and cannot be stirred away.

Broil: Broiling is the technique of cooking foods a measured distance from a direct source of heat. Both gas and electric ovens provide a means of broiling. Some rangetops have built-in grills that provide another broiling option. Grilling on a barbecue grill also fits this broad definition of broiling. The goal of broiling is to brown the exterior without overcooking the interior. Generally, the thinner the food item, the closer it should be to the heat source.

Brush: Brushing refers to the technique of applying a liquid such as melted butter, barbecue sauce, or glaze to the surface of food prior to or during cooking with a brush. It serves the same purpose as basting: preserving moistness, adding flavor, and giving foods an attractive appearance.

made by first beating egg whites, and then beating in sugar until stiff peaks form. Swiss meringue is made when egg whites and sugar are heated over simmering water, and then beaten until tall peaks form and the meringue is cold. Italian meringue is made when sugar syrup is cooked to the firm-ball stage, beaten into whipped egg whites, and then the whole mixture is whipped until cold.

SOUFFLÉ

A soufflé is a type of dish made with egg yolks, beaten egg whites, and a variety of other ingredients. Soufflés can be either sweet or savory and are often served as a dessert or main dish. The word soufflé is a form of the French verb *souffler*, which means "to blow up."

TORTE

A torte is a cake made with a number of eggs, ground nuts, or sometimes bread crumbs in the place of or in addition to all-purpose flour. Tortes originated in Central Europe, and the word torte was derived from the Italian word *torta*, which is used to describe a round cake.

Caramelize: Caramelizing is the technique of cooking sugar, sometimes with a small amount of water, to a very high temperature (between 310°F and 360°F) so that it melts into a clear brown liquid and develops a characteristic flavor. The color can vary from light golden brown to dark brown. Caramelized sugar, sometimes called "burnt sugar," is used in a variety of desserts and sauces.

Chill: Chilling is the technique of cooling foods, usually in the refrigerator or over ice, to a temperature of 35°F to 40°F. A recipe or dish may require several hours or as long as overnight to chill thoroughly. To chill a large portion of a hot mixture such as soup or chili, separate the mixture into several small containers for quicker cooling. To chill small amounts of hot food, place the food in a bowl or saucepan over a container of crushed ice or iced water or chill the food in the freezer for 20 to 30 minutes.

Chop: Chopping is the technique of cutting food into small, irregularly shaped pieces. Although the term does not designate a specific size, most cooks would suggest that food be chopped into approximately ¼-inch pieces. Chopped food is larger than minced food and more irregularly cut than diced food. Recipe directions may call for a coarsely chopped or a finely chopped ingredient.

Coat: To coat means to cover food with an outer layer, usually fine or powdery, using ingredients such as flour, crumbs, cornmeal, or sugar. With foods such as chicken, fish fillets, and eggplant, this coating is preliminary to frying or baking and provides a crispy exterior. Such foods are often first rolled in eggs or milk so the coating adheres. Some cookies are coated with sugar before or after baking.

Combine: Combining is the process of mixing two or more liquid or dry ingredients together to make them a uniform mixture.

Core: Coring means to remove the center seed-bearing structure of a fruit or vegetable. The most commonly cored foods are apples, pears, pineapple, zucchini, and cucumbers. First cutting the food into quarters and then cutting out the center core can accomplish coring with a small knife. A utensil specially designed to remove the core of specific whole fruits and vegetables is known as a corer. The most common corers are for apples, pears, and pineapple.

Combine

Cream: Creaming is the process of softening sugar and butter until the mixture is light or pale in color and well blended. Creaming can be done with a variety of baking tools including a wooden spoon, an electric mixer, or a food processor.

Crimp: To crimp means to seal two layers of dough together. This process can be done with either one's fingertips or a fork, and the term is most commonly used in reference to pie crusts. Depending upon the style of the pie, crimping can be used as a decorative finish for ornate desserts.

Crumble: To crumble means to break food into small pieces of irregular size. It is usually done with the fingers. Ingredients often crumbled include blue cheese and bacon. Both foods can be purchased in the supermarket already crumbled.

Crush: Crushing means reducing a food, such as crackers, to small fine particles by rolling with a rolling pin or pounding with a mortar and pestle. A food processor or blender also works well. Fruit can be crushed to extract its juices. Garlic is sometimes crushed with the flat side of a knife blade or garlic press to release its flavor.

Cutting In: Cutting in is the technique used to combine a chilled solid fat such as shortening or butter with dry ingredients such as flour so that the resulting mixture is in coarse, small pieces. A fork, two table knives, fingers, or a pastry blender may be used. If using a food processor, be careful not to over-mix the ingredients. This process is used to make biscuits, scones, pie pastry, and some cookies.

Dice: To dice is to cut food into small cubes that are uniform in size. The smallest dice, which is about ⅛ of an inch, is best suited for delicate garnishing. More typical are sizes between ¼ and ½ of an inch. Dicing is distinguished from chopping and mincing by the care taken to achieve a uniform size for an attractive presentation.

Dot: This term, generally used in cooking as "to dot with butter," refers to cutting butter (or margarine) into small bits and scattering them over a food. This technique allows the butter to melt evenly. It also keeps the food moist, adds richness, and can promote browning.

Crimp

Cutting In

Dust: Dusting is a technique used to lightly coat a food, before or after cooking, with a powdery ingredient such as flour or powdered sugar. The ingredient may be sprinkled on using your fingers or shaken from a small sieve or a container with holes on the top. A greased baking pan can be dusted with flour before it is filled, a technique also known as "flouring."

Flake: To flake refers to the technique of separating or breaking off small pieces or layers of a food using a utensil, such as a fork. For example, cooked fish fillets may be flaked for use in a salad or main dish.

Flour: To flour means to apply a light coating of flour to a food or piece of equipment. Applied to food, the flour dries the surface. This helps food brown better when frying or sautéing and keeps food such as raisins from sticking together. Baking pans are floured for better release characteristics and to produce thin, crisp crusts. Rolling pins, biscuit cutters, cookie cutters, and work surfaces are floured to prevent doughs from sticking to them.

Fold: Folding is a specialized technique for combining two ingredients or mixtures, one of which usually has been aerated, such as whipped cream or egg whites. It is best done by placing the airy mixture on top of the other and, with a rubber spatula, gently but quickly cutting through to the bottom, and turning the ingredients over with a rolling motion. The bowl is rotated a quarter-turn each time and the process repeated until the mixtures are combined with as little loss in volume as possible. Care must be taken not to stir, beat, or overmix. Fruit pieces, chips, or nuts may be folded into an airy mixture using the same technique.

Fry: Frying refers to the technique of cooking foods in hot fat, usually vegetable oil. Proper fat temperature is critical to a successful result. The ideal temperature produces a crisp exterior and a moist, perfectly cooked interior; too high a temperature will burn the food and too low a temperature will result in food absorbing excessive fat. A deep-fat thermometer is essential to determining the temperature of the fat. Deep-fried foods are submerged or floated in hot fat in a large heavy saucepan or Dutch oven. Electric deep fryers fitted with wire baskets are available. Pan-frying refers to cooking food in a skillet in a small amount of fat that does not cover the food.

Glaze: To glaze a dessert means to add a type of icing or topping that will give the dessert a smooth or shiny finishing coat. There are a number of different types of glazes. Pastry glazes, which are brushed onto dough before baking, are often made of egg, milk, and cream. Caramel and sieved jam can also be used as glazes.

Grate: Grating refers to the technique of making very small particles from a firm food like carrots, lemon peel, or Parmesan cheese by rubbing it along a coarse surface with small, sharp protrusions, usually a metal kitchen grater. Food may also be grated in a food processor using a specialized metal blade.

Grease: To grease a pan means to coat the inside surface of a pan or dish with a layer of fat. Butter, oil, and shortening are the most popular ingredients used for greasing, but recipes will often specify which type of fat to use. Pans can be greased using either a brush or kitchen paper.

Knead: Kneading refers to the technique of manipulating bread dough in order to develop the protein in flour, called gluten, to ensure the structure of the finished product. Kneading also aids in combining the dough ingredients. Biscuit dough is lightly kneaded—only about ten times—whereas yeast doughs may be vigorously kneaded for several minutes.

Level: Leveling refers to removing the crown, or rounded part, of a cake to create a flat surface conducive to frosting or decorating. The best way to level a cake is either with a sharp serrated knife or a tool called a cake leveler.

Mash: To mash is to crush a food into a soft, smooth mixture, as in mashed potatoes or bananas. It can be done with a tool called a potato masher or with an electric mixer. Small amounts of food, such as one or two bananas or a few hard-cooked egg yolks, can be mashed with a fork. For best results, make sure that potatoes are fully cooked so they are soft enough to become completely smooth.

Mince: Mincing refers to the technique of chopping food into very tiny, irregular pieces. Minced food is smaller than chopped food. Flavorful seasonings, such as garlic and fresh herbs, are often minced to distribute their flavor more evenly throughout a dish.

Glaze

Purée: To purée means to mash or strain a soft or cooked food until it has a smooth consistency. This can be done with a food processor, sieve, blender, or food mill. For best results, the food must be naturally soft, such as raspberries or ripe pears, or cooked until it is completely tender. Puréed foods are used as sauces and as ingredients in other sweet or savory dishes. The term also refers to the foods that result from the process.

Proof: Proofing is the process by which dough expands and rises, and it is called for in all yeast bread recipes. Dough proofs when it sits in a warm spot, free from draft, for several hours. The dough rises during the proofing process because the yeast ferments, which produces carbon dioxide.

Reduce: To reduce is to boil a liquid until its volume has been decreased through evaporation. This results in a more intense flavor and thicker consistency. Typically, reduced sauces are ⅓ or ½ of their original volume. Use a pan with a wide bottom to shorten preparation time. The reduced product is referred to as a "reduction." Since the flavor of the seasonings will also become concentrated when a sauce is reduced, add the seasonings to the sauce after it has been reduced.

Roll Out

Roll Out: To roll out means to flatten dough into an even layer using a rolling pin. To roll out pastry or cookie dough, place the dough—which should be in the shape of a disc—on a floured surface, such as a counter, pastry cloth, or a large cutting board. Lightly flour your hands and the rolling pin. Place the rolling pin across the center of the dough. With several light strokes, roll the rolling pin away from you toward the edge of the dough. Turn the dough a quarter-turn and roll again from the center to the edge. Repeat this process until the dough is the desired thickness. If the dough becomes sticky, dust it and the rolling pin with flour. If the dough sticks to the surface, gently fold back the edge of the dough and dust the surface underneath the dough with flour.

Scald: To scald means to heat some type of liquid, usually a dairy product such as cream, in a saucepan until it is almost boiling. Tiny bubbles around the perimeter of the pan are often a good indicator that the liquid has reached the scalding stage. Scalded milk is often essential to custards, pudding, and sauce recipes.

Sift: Sifting is the technique of passing a dry ingredient such as flour or powdered sugar through the fine mesh of a sieve or sifter for the purpose of breaking up lumps and making it lighter in texture. Sifting results in finer baked goods and smoother frostings. Most all-purpose flour is pre-sifted, eliminating the need for sifting. Cake flour is generally sifted before using. Spoon the ingredient into the sieve and push it through the mesh screen using a metal spoon or rubber spatula.

Simmer: To simmer is to cook a liquid or a food in a liquid with gentle heat just below the boiling point. Small bubbles slowly rising to the surface of the liquid indicate simmering.

Sliver: To sliver is the technique of cutting food into thin strips or pieces. Basil and garlic are two ingredients that may be identified as slivered in a recipe. The word "sliver" may also refer to a long, thin strip of food or a small wedge of a pie.

Strain: Straining refers to the technique of pouring a liquid through the small holes of a strainer or the wire mesh of a sieve to remove lumps or unwanted particles.

Temper: In baking terms, temper has two different meanings. The first meaning is a process that calls for the heating and then cooling of chocolate. This process ensures that chocolate will be firm when it reaches room temperature. Tempering also refers to the process of adding egg yolks to a hot sauce without curdling; the egg yolks are gently heated, then a small amount of the sauce is added to the yolks and the mixture is beaten well.

Toast: Toasting is the technique of browning foods by means of dry heat. Bread products, nuts, seeds, and coconut are commonly toasted. Toasting is done in a toaster, toaster oven, oven, or skillet, or under the broiler. The purpose of toasting bread is to brown, crisp, and dry it. Nuts, seeds, and coconut are toasted to intensify their flavor.

Whip: To whip refers to the technique of beating ingredients such as egg whites and whipping cream with a wire whisk or electric mixer in order to incorporate air and increase their volume. This results in a light, fluffy texture.

Whisk: Whisking is the technique of stirring, beating, or whipping foods with a wire whisk. If you do not have a whisk, you can use a wooden spoon if the purpose is to blend ingredients. For whipping foods, an electric mixer can be used instead.

Sift

Sliver

Bars and Brownies

A mouthwatering collection of classic and contemporary handheld treats

Key Lime Bars

MAKES 24 BARS

- 1½ **cups finely crushed graham crackers (about 10 to 12 crackers)**
- 4 **tablespoons packed brown sugar**
- 2 **tablespoons all-purpose flour**
- 5 **tablespoons melted butter**
- 8 **ounces cream cheese, softened**
- 1½ **cups granulated sugar**
- 2 **eggs**
- ¼ **cup freshly squeezed Key lime juice**
- 1 **tablespoon grated lime peel**

1. Preheat oven to 350°F and grease 13×9-inch baking pan; set aside.

2. Combine graham cracker crumbs, brown sugar and flour in large bowl. Add melted butter to cracker mixture in 2 parts, stirring until mixture is thoroughly moist and crumbly.

3. Reserve ¼ cup crumbs to top bars, if desired. Press crust evenly into bottom of pan and bake 15 minutes; set aside.

4. Place cream cheese and granulated sugar in bowl of electric stand mixer. Beat at medium-low speed until smooth and creamy. Add eggs, 1 at a time, beating well after each addition. Add lime juice and lime peel. Mix until just combined.

5. Pour filling over warm crust. Bake in center of oven 15 to 20 minutes or until filling is set and begins to separate from sides of pan.

6. Sprinkle reserved crust crumbs evenly over filling, if desired. Cool on wire rack 2 hours. Using sharp knife, cut into 2-inch bars.

Orange Marmalade Bars

Shortbread Crust

- ¼ cup hazelnuts, roasted, husks removed
- 1 cup all-purpose flour
- ¼ cup packed brown sugar
- 6 tablespoons butter
- 1 egg
- 1 teaspoon vanilla

Filling

- 1 cup plus 2 teaspoons orange marmalade, divided
- 4 ounces cream cheese
- ¼ cup heavy cream
- 1 tablespoon granulated sugar
- 1 tablespoon grated orange peel
- ½ cup hazelnuts, roasted, husks removed
- 2 tablespoons packed brown sugar
- 1 teaspoon all-purpose flour
- 2 tablespoons melted butter

1. Preheat oven to 375°F. Grease 13×9-inch baking pan.

2. For crust, grind hazelnuts in food processor. Place in large bowl and whisk together with flour and brown sugar. Using pastry blender or 2 knives, cut butter into dry ingredients until mixture resembles coarse meal. Add egg and vanilla; stir just until dough forms.

3. Press dough evenly into pan to form crust. Bake 12 to 15 minutes or until crust is golden brown.

4. Spread 1 cup marmalade evenly across hot crust.

5. Place cream cheese, cream, granulated sugar, remaining 2 teaspoons marmalade and orange peel in bowl of electric stand mixer. Mix on low speed until smooth and creamy. Finely chop hazelnuts. Toss nuts with brown sugar, flour and butter until nuts are evenly coated.

6. Pour cream cheese mixture over marmalade and crust. Sprinkle hazelnut topping evenly over filling. Bake 12 to 15 minutes or until topping is lightly browned and filling bubbles slightly.

7. Cool on wire rack 2 hours. Use sharp knife to cut into 2-inch bars.

Sweet Potato Coconut Bars

MAKES 24 BARS

30 vanilla wafers, finely crushed

1½ cups finely chopped walnuts, toasted, divided

½ cup sweetened flaked coconut, plus additional for topping

¼ cup (½ stick) butter, softened

2 cans (16 ounces each) sweet potatoes, well drained and mashed (2 cups total)

2 eggs

1 teaspoon ground cinnamon

½ teaspoon ground ginger

¼ to ½ teaspoon ground cloves

¼ teaspoon salt

1 can (14 ounces) sweetened condensed milk

1 cup butterscotch chips

1. Preheat oven to 350°F.

2. For crust, combine vanilla wafers, 1 cup walnuts, coconut and butter in medium bowl until well blended. (Mixture will be dry and crumbly.) Place two thirds of mixture in bottom of 13×9-inch baking pan, pressing down lightly to form even layer.

3. For filling, beat mashed sweet potatoes, eggs, cinnamon, ginger, cloves and salt in bowl of electric stand mixer at medium-low speed until well blended. Gradually add milk; beat until well blended. Spoon filling evenly over crust. Top with remaining crumb mixture, pressing lightly into sweet potato layer.

4. Bake 25 to 30 minutes or until knife inserted into center comes out clean. Sprinkle with butterscotch chips, remaining ½ cup walnuts and additional coconut. Bake 2 minutes more. Cool completely in pan on wire rack. Cover with plastic wrap and refrigerate 2 to 3 hours before serving.

Caramel Chocolate Chunk Blondies

MAKES 30 BARS

1½ cups all-purpose flour

1 teaspoon baking powder

½ teaspoon salt

½ cup (1 stick) butter, softened

¾ cup granulated sugar

¾ cup packed brown sugar

2 eggs

1½ teaspoons vanilla

1½ cups semisweet chocolate chunks

⅓ cup homemade or store-bought caramel topping

1. Preheat oven to 350°F. Spray 13×9-inch baking pan with nonstick cooking spray.

2. Combine flour, baking powder and salt in medium bowl; set aside. Place butter, granulated sugar and brown sugar in bowl of electric stand mixer. Beat until smooth and creamy. Beat in eggs and vanilla until well blended. Add flour mixture; beat until blended. Stir in chocolate chunks.

3. Spread batter evenly in prepared pan. Drop spoonfuls of caramel topping over batter; swirl caramel into batter with knife.

4. Bake 25 minutes or until golden brown. Cool in pan on wire rack.

Mocha Fudge Brownies

MAKES 16 BROWNIES

- 3 squares (1 ounce each) semisweet chocolate
- ¾ cup sugar
- ½ cup (1 stick) butter, softened
- 2 eggs
- 2 teaspoons instant espresso powder
- 1 teaspoon vanilla
- ½ cup all-purpose flour
- ½ cup chopped toasted almonds
- 1 cup (6 ounces) milk chocolate chips, divided

1. Preheat oven to 350°F. Grease 8-inch square baking pan.

2. Melt semisweet chocolate in top of double boiler over hot, not boiling, water. Remove from heat; let cool slightly.

3. Beat sugar and butter in bowl of electric stand mixer at low speed until well blended. Add eggs; beat until light and fluffy. Add melted chocolate, espresso powder and vanilla; beat until well blended. Stir in flour, almonds and ½ cup chocolate chips. Spread batter evenly in prepared pan.

4. Bake 25 minutes or just until firm in center. Remove from oven; sprinkle with remaining ½ cup chocolate chips. Let stand until chips melt; spread chocolate evenly over brownies. Cool completely in pan on wire rack. Cut into 2-inch squares.

Pear Hazelnut Bars

MAKES 36 BARS

1 recipe Basic Shortbread Dough (recipe follows)

1 tablespoon plus 1 teaspoon grated lemon peel, divided

4 cups chopped, peeled fresh pears

½ cup raisins

2 tablespoons lemon juice

2 tablespoons all-purpose flour

2 tablespoons granulated sugar

½ teaspoon ground cinnamon

Crumb Topping

½ cup all-purpose flour

½ cup packed brown sugar

½ teaspoon ground cinnamon

½ cup (1 stick) cold butter, cubed

½ cup old-fashioned oats

½ cup chopped hazelnuts

1. Preheat oven to 350°F. Line 13×9-inch baking pan with foil, leaving 1-inch overhang. Spray foil with nonstick cooking spray.

2. Prepare Basic Shortbread Dough, adding 1 tablespoon lemon peel to butter and sugar mixture. Press dough evenly into pan. Bake 25 minutes or until lightly browned. Set pan aside on wire rack.

3. Meanwhile, mix pears, raisins, lemon juice, 2 tablespoons flour, granulated sugar, cinnamon and remaining 1 teaspoon lemon peel in large bowl. Arrange over warm crust.

4. For topping, combine ½ cup flour, brown sugar and cinnamon in medium bowl. Cut in butter with pastry blender or 2 knives until mixture resembles coarse crumbs. Stir in oats and hazelnuts. Sprinkle topping evenly over filling, lightly pressing into place.

5. Bake 30 to 32 minutes or until topping is bubbly and golden brown. Cool completely on wire rack.

6. Refrigerate bars at least 2 hours before serving. Remove foil from bars; cut into squares. Cut each square diagonally into triangles. Store covered in refrigerator.

Basic Shortbread Dough

¾ cup (1½ sticks) butter, slightly softened

¾ cup sugar

3 egg yolks

1 teaspoon vanilla

2 cups all-purpose flour

¼ teaspoon salt

Beat butter and sugar in bowl of electric stand mixer at medium speed 1 minute. Beat in egg yolks and vanilla until well blended. Scrape down bowl. Add flour and salt all at once; mix until just combined. Use immediately according to selected recipe or shape into 2 discs; wrap in plastic and refrigerate. Dough will keep in refrigerator up to 3 days, or may be frozen up to 1 month.

Cranberry Coconut Bars

MAKES 24 BARS

Filling

2 cups fresh or frozen cranberries

1 cup dried sweetened cranberries

⅔ cup granulated sugar

¼ cup water

Grated peel of 1 lemon

Crust

1¼ cups all-purpose flour

¾ cup old-fashioned oats

½ teaspoon baking soda

½ teaspoon salt

¾ cup (1½ sticks) unsalted butter, softened

1 cup firmly packed light brown sugar

1 cup chopped toasted pecans*

1 cup sweetened flaked coconut

To toast pecans, spread in single layer on baking sheet. Bake in preheated 350°F oven 5 to 7 minutes or until golden brown, stirring frequently.

1. Preheat oven to 400°F. Grease and flour 13×9-inch baking pan.

2. For filling, combine fresh cranberries, dried cranberries, granulated sugar, water and lemon peel in medium saucepan. Cook 10 to 15 minutes over medium-high heat until mixture is pulpy, stirring frequently. Mash cranberries with back of spoon. Cool to lukewarm.

3. For crust, combine flour, oats, baking soda and salt in medium bowl; set aside. Beat butter and brown sugar in bowl of electric stand mixer at medium speed until creamy. Add flour mixture; beat just until blended. Stir in pecans and coconut. Reserve 1½ cups; pat remaining crumb mixture in bottom of prepared pan. Bake 10 minutes; remove from oven.

4. Gently spread cranberry filling evenly over crust. Sprinkle with reserved crumb mixture. Bake 18 to 20 minutes or until bars are set and crust is golden brown. Cool completely before cutting into bars.

Note: You can make these bars when fresh or frozen cranberries aren't available. Prepare the filling using 2 cups dried sweetened cranberries, 1 cup water and peel of 1 lemon; cook 8 to 10 minutes over medium heat, stirring frequently. Use as directed in step 4.

Dark Chocolate Nut Bars

MAKES 48 BARS

- 1 **package (12 ounces) dark chocolate nuggets with almonds***
- 1½ **cups all-purpose flour**
- ⅓ **cup unsweetened Dutch process cocoa powder**
- 1½ **teaspoons baking powder**
- ½ **teaspoon salt**
- 1 **cup (2 sticks) butter, softened**
- ¾ **cup packed brown sugar**
- ½ **cup granulated sugar**
- 2 **eggs**
- 1 **teaspoon vanilla**
- 1 **cup chopped pecans**

Or substitute your favorite candy bar, enough to make 1½ cups chopped candy.

1. Preheat oven to 350°F. Grease 13×9-inch baking pan. Chop candy into ¼-inch chunks; place in refrigerator until ready to use.

2. Combine flour, cocoa, baking powder and salt in small bowl; set aside. Beat butter, brown sugar and granulated sugar in bowl of electric stand mixer until creamy. Beat in eggs and vanilla until well blended. Stir in flour mixture.

3. Reserve half of chopped candy; stir remaining candy and pecans into dough. Spread dough in prepared pan. Sprinkle with reserved candy.

4. Bake about 25 minutes or until toothpick inserted into center comes out clean. Cut into 1½-inch squares.

Chocolate Raspberry Bars

1. Preheat oven to 350°F. Grease 9-inch square baking pan.

2. Combine flour, oats, cocoa, baking powder, salt and baking soda in medium bowl; set aside. Place brown sugar and butter in bowl of electric stand mixer. Beat at medium speed until smooth and creamy. Beat in eggs until well blended. Add flour mixture; beat until blended. Stir in chocolate candies.

3. Reserve 1 cup dough. Spread remaining dough in prepared pan. Spread preserves evenly over dough to within ½ inch of edges of pan. Drop teaspoonfuls of reserved dough over preserves.

4. Bake 25 to 30 minutes or until bars are slightly firm near edges. Cool completely on wire rack.

MAKES 16 BARS

1⅓ **cups all-purpose flour**

1 **cup quick oats**

⅓ **cup unsweetened cocoa powder**

1 **teaspoon baking powder**

½ **teaspoon salt**

¼ **teaspoon baking soda**

1 **cup packed brown sugar**

½ **cup (1 stick) butter, softened**

2 **eggs**

1 **cup mini candy-coated chocolate pieces**

⅓ **cup seedless raspberry jam**

Fudge Brownies

1   cup (2 sticks) butter, softened, divided

4   squares (1 ounce each) unsweetened chocolate

2   cups sugar

1   teaspoon vanilla

3   eggs

1   cup all-purpose flour

½   teaspoon salt

1   cup chopped walnuts or pecans

1. Melt ½ cup butter and chocolate in small saucepan over low heat; set aside to cool.

2. Place remaining ½ cup butter, sugar and vanilla in bowl of electric stand mixer. Attach flat beater to mixer. Turn to low and mix about 30 seconds. Turn to medium and beat about 2 minutes. Turn to medium-low. Add eggs, 1 at a time, beating about 15 seconds after each addition. Stop and scrape bowl.

3. Add cooled chocolate mixture. Turn to low and mix 30 seconds. Stop and scrape bowl. Add all remaining ingredients. Turn to low and mix until well blended, about 30 seconds.

4. Pour into greased and floured 13×9×2-inch baking pan. Bake at 350°F for 45 minutes. Cool in pan on wire rack.

Spiked Cheesecake Bars

1. Preheat oven to 350°F. Line bottom and sides of 8-inch square baking pan with foil, leaving 2-inch overhang.

2. For crust, beat brown sugar and butter in bowl of electric stand mixer at medium-high speed until creamy. Combine ¾ cup flour, oats and baking soda in small bowl; gradually beat into sugar mixture at low speed until blended. (Mixture will be crumbly.) Lightly press mixture into bottom of prepared pan to form crust. Bake 20 to 25 minutes or until golden brown. Set aside on wire rack.

3. Meanwhile, for filling, combine cream cheese, granulated sugar, liqueur and milk in mixer bowl. Beat at medium-high speed until smooth. Add egg and remaining 1 teaspoon flour; beat until well blended. Spoon filling over hot crust. Bake 38 to 43 minutes or until set. Cool completely in pan on wire rack.

4. Place chocolate chips in small resealable food storage bag; microwave on HIGH 1 minute or until slightly melted. Knead bag; microwave 20 seconds or until completely melted. Cut tiny hole in 1 corner of bag and drizzle chocolate over cooled cheesecake. Cover with foil and refrigerate overnight for best flavor and texture. Before cutting, remove cheesecake from pan using foil handles; place on cutting board.

MAKES 24 BARS

- ½ **cup packed light brown sugar**
- ⅓ **cup butter, softened**
- ¾ **cup plus 1 teaspoon all-purpose flour, divided**
- ¾ **cup quick oats**
- ¼ **teaspoon baking soda**
- 1 **package (8 ounces) cream cheese, softened**
- ¼ **cup granulated sugar**
- ¼ **cup any flavored liqueur, such as coffee, orange or hazelnut**
- 2 **tablespoons milk**
- 1 **egg**
- ¼ **cup semisweet chocolate chips**

Carrot and Spice Bars

MAKES 40 BARS

- 1 **cup low-fat (1%) milk**
- ¼ **cup butter**
- 1 **cup bran flakes cereal**
- 2 **eggs**
- 1 **jar (2½ ounces) puréed baby food carrots**
- ¾ **cup grated carrot**
- ⅓ **cup golden raisins, coarsely chopped**
- 1 **teaspoon grated orange peel**
- 1 **teaspoon vanilla**
- 2 **cups all-purpose flour**
- ¾ **cup sugar**
- 1 **teaspoon baking soda**
- 1 **teaspoon ground cinnamon**
- ¼ **cup orange juice**
- ¼ **cup toasted pecans, chopped**

1. Preheat oven to 350°F. Lightly coat 13×9-inch baking pan with nonstick cooking spray; set aside.

2. Combine milk and butter in large microwaveable bowl. Microwave on HIGH 1 minute or until butter is melted; add cereal. Let stand 5 minutes. Add eggs; whisk to blend. Add puréed carrots, grated carrot, raisins, orange peel and vanilla.

3. Combine flour, sugar, baking soda and cinnamon in medium bowl. Add to carrot mixture, stirring until thoroughly blended. Spread into prepared pan.

4. Bake 25 minutes or until toothpick inserted in center comes out clean. Insert tines of fork into cake at 1-inch intervals. Spoon orange juice over cake. Sprinkle with pecans; press into cake. Cut into 40 bars before serving.

Chunky Caramel Nut Brownies

1. Preheat oven to 350°F. Grease 13×9-inch baking pan.

2. Place butter and chocolate in large microwaveable bowl. Microwave on HIGH 1½ to 2 minutes or until chocolate is melted and mixture is smooth when stirred. Pour mixture into bowl of electric stand mixer. Turn mixer to low and mix in sugar until well blended. Beat in eggs, 1 at a time. Add flour; mix on low until well blended. Spread half of batter in prepared pan. Bake 20 minutes.

3. Meanwhile, combine caramels and cream in medium microwaveable bowl. Microwave on HIGH 1½ to 2 minutes or until caramels begin to melt; stir until mixture is smooth. Stir in 1 cup pecan halves.

4. Spread caramel mixture over partially baked brownie base. Sprinkle with half of chocolate chunks. Pour remaining brownie batter over top; sprinkle with remaining 1 cup pecan halves and chocolate chunks. Bake 25 to 30 minutes or until set. Cool completely in pan on wire rack. Cut into squares.

MAKES 24 BARS

- ¾ cup (1½ sticks) butter
- 4 squares (1 ounce each) unsweetened chocolate
- 2 cups sugar
- 4 eggs
- 1 cup all-purpose flour
- 1 package (14 ounces) caramels
- ¼ cup whipping cream
- 2 cups pecan halves or coarsely chopped pecans, divided
- 1 package (12 ounces) chocolate chunks or chips

Gingerbread Cheesecake Bars

MAKES 24 BARS

- 1 package (8 ounces) cream cheese, softened
- ⅔ cup granulated sugar, divided
- 3 eggs, divided
- ½ teaspoon vanilla
- 1½ teaspoons ground ginger, divided
- ½ cup (1 stick) butter, softened
- ¾ cup molasses
- 2 cups all-purpose flour
- 1 teaspoon baking soda
- ¾ teaspoon ground cinnamon
- ¼ teaspoon salt
- ¼ teaspoon ground allspice

1. Preheat oven to 350°F. Grease 13×9-inch baking pan.

2. Beat cream cheese and ⅓ cup sugar in bowl of electric stand mixer at medium speed until light and fluffy. Add 1 egg, vanilla and ½ teaspoon ginger; beat until well blended and smooth. Refrigerate until ready to use. Clean mixer bowl.

3. Place butter and remaining ⅓ cup sugar in bowl of electric stand mixer. Beat at medium speed until light and fluffy. Add molasses and remaining 2 eggs; beat until well blended. Combine flour, baking soda, remaining 1 teaspoon ginger, cinnamon, salt and allspice in separate bowl. Add flour mixture to butter mixture; beat just until blended. Spread batter evenly in prepared pan. Drop cream cheese mixture by spoonfuls onto gingerbread batter; swirl into batter with knife.

4. Bake 25 to 30 minutes or until toothpick inserted into center comes out clean. Cool completely on wire rack.

Gooey Chocolate Caramel Bars

1. Preheat oven to 350°F. Line 13×9-inch baking pan with foil. Combine flour, granulated sugar and salt in medium bowl. Cut in 14 tablespoons (1¾ sticks) butter until mixture resembles coarse crumbs. Press into bottom of prepared pan.

2. Bake 18 to 20 minutes or until lightly browned around edges. Remove pan to wire rack; cool completely.

3. Combine 1 cup (2 sticks) butter, brown sugar and corn syrup in heavy medium saucepan. Cook over medium heat 5 to 8 minutes or until mixture boils, stirring frequently. Boil gently 2 minutes without stirring. Immediately pour over cooled base; spread evenly to edges of pan. Cool completely.

4. Melt chocolate and remaining 2 tablespoons butter in double boiler over hot (not boiling) water. Pour over caramel layer; spread evenly to edges of pan. Refrigerate 10 to 15 minutes or until chocolate begins to set. Remove; cool completely. Cut into bars.

MAKES 36 BARS

- 2 **cups all-purpose flour**
- 1 **cup granulated sugar**
- ¼ **teaspoon salt**
- 2 **cups (4 sticks) butter, divided**
- 1 **cup packed light brown sugar**
- ⅓ **cup light corn syrup**
- 1 **cup (6 ounces) semisweet chocolate chips**

tip

Use a very sharp knife to cut bars into squares. Because the caramel layer may be sticky, wipe the knife blade clean between each slice.

Cappuccino Crunch Bars

MAKES 30 BARS

1¾ cups all-purpose flour, sifted

1 teaspoon baking soda

1 teaspoon salt

½ teaspoon ground cinnamon

1½ cups packed brown sugar

1 cup (2 sticks) butter, softened

½ cup granulated sugar

2 eggs

2 teaspoons instant coffee granules or espresso powder, dissolved in 1 tablespoon hot water and cooled to room temperature

2 teaspoons vanilla

1 teaspoon grated orange peel (optional)

1 cup white chocolate chips

1 cup chocolate-covered toffee baking bits

1. Preheat oven to 350°F. Grease 13×9-inch baking pan.

2. Combine flour, baking soda, salt and cinnamon in large bowl; set aside. Place brown sugar, butter and granulated sugar in bowl of electric stand mixer. Beat at medium speed until fluffy. Add eggs, 1 at a time, beating well after each addition. Add coffee mixture, vanilla and orange peel, if desired; beat well. Add flour mixture; beat until well blended. Stir in white chocolate chips and toffee bits.

3. Spread batter evenly in prepared pan. Bake 25 to 35 minutes or until center is firm to the touch. Cool completely in pan on wire rack. Cut into bars.

Morning Sandwiches

1. Preheat oven to 425°F. Spray 13×9-inch baking pan with nonstick cooking spray; set aside.

2. Melt butter in small nonstick saucepan over medium heat. Add oats and almonds; cook and stir 3 minutes. Remove from heat and let cool.

3. Place oat mixture, flour, apple, carrots, egg substitute, prunes, milk, sugar substitute, baking powder, cinnamon, baking soda and nutmeg in food processor; pulse until combined.

4. Press dough evenly into prepared pan. Bake 20 minutes. Cool 15 minutes in pan on wire rack.

5. Cut into 12 pieces. Spread 6 pieces with peanut butter. Spread remaining 6 bars with raspberry preserves. Top raspberry bars with peanut butter bars to make sandwiches.

MAKES 6 BARS

- 1 tablespoon butter or vegetable oil
- ¾ cup quick oats
- ¼ cup sliced almonds
- 1 cup whole wheat flour
- 1 cup peeled and grated apple
- 1 cup shredded carrots
- ⅓ cup cholesterol-free egg substitute
- ¼ cup pitted and chopped prunes
- ¼ cup fat-free (skim) milk
- 2 tablespoons sugar substitute
- ½ teaspoon baking powder
- ½ teaspoon ground cinnamon
- ¼ teaspoon baking soda
- ¼ teaspoon ground nutmeg
- 6 teaspoons reduced-fat peanut butter
- 6 teaspoons sugar-free raspberry preserves

Aztec Brownies

- 1 package (12 ounces) semisweet chocolate chips
- 1 cup (2 sticks) butter, softened
- 1 cup sugar
- 3 eggs
- 1 tablespoon instant espresso powder
- 1 tablespoon vanilla
- ¾ cup all-purpose flour
- 2 teaspoons baking powder
- 1 teaspoon ground cinnamon
- 1 to 2 teaspoons chili powder
- ½ teaspoon salt
- ¾ cup sliced almonds

1. Preheat oven to 350°F. Spray 13×9-inch baking pan with nonstick cooking spray. Line pan with foil and spray foil.

2. Place chocolate chips and butter in medium microwaveable bowl; microwave on HIGH 30 seconds. Stir until mixture is smooth. (If lumps remain, microwave 10 seconds more and stir again.)

3. Whisk sugar, eggs, espresso powder and vanilla in medium bowl until well blended. Stir in warm chocolate mixture; set aside to cool 10 minutes. Whisk flour, baking powder, cinnamon, chili powder and salt in large bowl; stir in chocolate mixture until well blended. Pour into prepared pan.

4. Bake 15 minutes; remove pan from oven and sprinkle with almonds. Bake 20 minutes longer or until top is no longer shiny and toothpick inserted into center comes out almost clean. (Do not overbake.) Cool completely in pan on wire rack before cutting into squares or triangles.

Shortbread Turtle Cookie Bars

1. Preheat oven to 350°F.

2. Beat ½ cup butter in bowl of electric stand mixer at medium speed 2 minutes or until light and fluffy. Add flour, oats, ¾ cup brown sugar, cinnamon and salt; beat at low speed until coarse crumbs form. Pat firmly into bottom of ungreased 13×9-inch baking pan. Set aside.

3. Heat remaining ¾ cup butter and ¾ cup brown sugar in heavy medium saucepan over medium-high heat, stirring constantly until butter melts. Bring mixture to a boil; cook 1 minute without stirring. Remove from heat; stir in pecans. Pour over crust.

4. Bake 18 to 22 minutes on center rack of oven or until caramel begins to bubble. Immediately sprinkle with white chocolate, peanut butter chips and bittersweet chocolate; swirl (do not spread) with knife after 45 seconds to 1 minute or when slightly softened. Cool completely in pan on wire rack. Cut into 2×1-inch bars.

MAKES 54 BARS

- 1¼ cups (2½ sticks) butter, softened, divided
- 1 cup all-purpose flour
- 1 cup old-fashioned oats
- 1½ cups packed brown sugar, divided
- 1 teaspoon ground cinnamon
- ¼ teaspoon salt
- 1½ cups chopped pecans
- 4 squares (1 ounce each) white chocolate, finely chopped
- 1 cup peanut butter chips
- 6 squares (1 ounce each) bittersweet or semisweet chocolate, finely chopped

Breads

Cinnamon Raisin Bread

MAKES 2 LOAVES

- 4 **cups all-purpose flour**
- 2½ **teaspoons salt**
- 2½ **teaspoons active dry yeast**
- 4 **tablespoons (½ stick) butter plus 2 tablespoons melted butter, divided**
- 1 **cup plus 2 tablespoons milk**
- 2 **tablespoons honey**
- 2 **eggs**
- 1 **cup raisins**
- 8 **teaspoons sugar**
- 4 **teaspoons ground cinnamon**

1. Combine flour, salt and yeast in bowl of electric stand mixer. Melt 4 tablespoons butter in saucepan over low heat; stir in milk and honey until mixture is warm but not hot. Add eggs and whisk to combine; remove from heat.

2. Attach dough hook to mixer. Pour wet ingredients and raisins over dry ingredients. Turn mixer to low and stir until dough separates from sides of bowl and forms a ball. Knead on low about 2 minutes longer.

3. Place dough in lightly oiled bowl covered with plastic wrap. Set in warm place and let rise 1 to 1½ hours or until dough is doubled in bulk.

4. Punch down dough and separate into 2 balls. Shape each ball into 8×10×½-inch rectangle. Brush tops of dough with 1 tablespoon melted butter.

5. Combine sugar and cinnamon in small bowl. Set aside 2 teaspoons of mixture; spread remaining mixture evenly across dough.

6. Roll up each slab of dough and pat to shape into loaves. Place loaves in lightly greased and floured loaf pans. Cover with plastic wrap. Let rise 1 to 1½ hours.

7. Bake loaves at 375°F for 35 minutes, turning once to ensure even baking. Loaves should be golden brown and internal temperature should register 180°F. Brush tops with remaining 1 tablespoon melted butter; sprinkle with reserved cinnamon-sugar mixture. Cool 10 minutes. Remove bread from loaf pans; cool completely on wire racks.

Egg Bagels

MAKES 12 BAGELS

½ to ¾ cup warm water
  (105°F to 115°F), divided

1 package (¼ ounce) active
  dry yeast

2 tablespoons plus 1 teaspoon
  sugar

2½ cups all-purpose flour

1 tablespoon canola oil

1 teaspoon salt

2 eggs, divided

2 quarts water

2 tablespoons cold water

tip

For variety, consider adding toasted chopped onions, Kosher salt, sesame seeds, or poppy seeds to bagels. Add toppings after brushing with egg mixture, just before baking.

1. Combine ¼ cup warm water, yeast and 1 teaspoon sugar in medium bowl. Stir to dissolve yeast and let stand until bubbly, about 5 minutes.

2. Place flour, oil and salt in bowl of electric stand mixer. Attach dough hook to mixer. Turn to low and mix 1 minute or until combined. Add yeast mixture and 1 egg; mix until blended, about 1 minute.

3. With mixer running, very slowly drizzle dough with just enough warm water so dough forms ball that cleans sides of bowl. Knead on low 2 minutes more. Turn off mixer and let dough stand 1 to 2 minutes.

4. Turn mixer to low and gradually drizzle in enough remaining warm water to make dough soft, smooth and satiny but not sticky. Knead on low about 2 minutes longer.

5. Turn dough onto lightly greased surface. Shape into ball and cover with plastic wrap. Let stand about 15 minutes.

6. Divide dough into 12 equal pieces. Shape each piece into 1 strand about 6 inches long. Bring both ends of each strand together to form a doughnut shape. Moisten ends and pinch together to seal. Place bagels on greased cookie sheet. Let stand at room temperature 15 minutes.

7. Combine 2 quarts water and remaining 2 tablespoons sugar in Dutch oven. Bring water to a boil. Gently place 3 or 4 bagels at a time in boiling water. When bagels rise to the surface, turn them over and cook until puffy, 1½ to 2 minutes longer. Remove bagels from water with slotted spoon and place on greased cookie sheet.

8. Heat oven to 425°F. Beat remaining egg and 2 tablespoons cold water with fork. Brush mixture over bagels. Bake until crusts are golden and crisp, 20 to 25 minutes. Remove from cookie sheet. Cool on wire rack.

Soft Beer Pretzels

MAKES 12 PRETZELS

3¼ cups all-purpose flour, divided

1 package rapid-rise yeast

1 teaspoon salt

⅔ cup beer

6½ cups water, divided

2 tablespoons vegetable oil

2 tablespoons baking soda

1 egg, beaten

Kosher salt

tip

When shaping pretzels, make large exaggerated loops. Smaller loops will close when boiled.

1. Combine 3 cups flour, yeast and salt in bowl of electric stand mixer. In medium saucepan, heat beer, ½ cup water and oil to 120°F. Add beer mixture to flour mixture. Turn mixer to medium-low; beat until moistened. Stir in enough remaining flour, 1 tablespoon at a time, to form soft dough. Turn dough onto lightly floured surface; knead 5 to 6 minutes or until smooth and elastic. Cover and let rise in warm place 15 minutes.

2. Divide dough in half, and then divide each half into 6 pieces. With lightly floured hands, roll each piece into 1 (14-inch) rope with tapered ends. (Cover remaining dough while working to prevent it from drying out.) Form pretzel by creating a U shape, then cross 1 end over the other to form a circle, leaving about 3 inches at the end of each rope. Twist rope at base of circle and fold ends over circle to form pretzel shape. Place on greased baking sheets. Cover and let rise in warm place 15 minutes.

3. Preheat oven to 400°F. In large non-aluminum pot, bring 6 cups water to a boil; stir in baking soda. Working in batches, gently lower pretzels into boiling water; cook 30 seconds, turning once. Using a slotted spoon, remove pretzels to wire rack coated with nonstick cooking spray.

4. Brush pretzels with beaten egg and sprinkle with salt. Bake on ungreased baking sheet 10 minutes or until golden brown. Cool on wire rack.

Herb Garlic Baguettes

1 package active dry yeast

1 teaspoon sugar

¼ cup warm water (105°F to 115°F)

3¼ to 3½ cups all-purpose flour

1 tablespoon chopped fresh basil or 1 teaspoon dried basil

2 teaspoons chopped fresh oregano or ½ teaspoon dried oregano

2 teaspoons chopped fresh thyme or ½ teaspoon dried thyme

1 teaspoon fresh minced garlic

1 teaspoon salt

¾ cup cold water

1 egg

1 teaspoon water

1. Dissolve yeast and sugar in warm water.

2. Place 3¼ cups flour, basil, oregano, thyme, garlic and salt in bowl of electric stand mixer. Attach dough hook to mixer. Turn to low and mix 30 seconds. Stop and scrape bowl. Continuing on low, slowly add yeast mixture and cold water, mixing about 30 seconds. If dough is sticky, add remaining ¼ cup flour. Knead on low until dough is smooth and elastic, about 3 minutes.

3. Cover; let rise at room temperature (70°F to 80°F), free from draft, until doubled in size, 1½ to 2 hours.

4. On lightly floured surface, punch dough down several times to remove all air bubbles, and divide dough in half. Shape each half into 12-inch-long loaf. Place each loaf on greased baking sheet or in greased baguette pan. With sharp knife, make 3 to 4 shallow diagonal slashes in top of dough. Combine egg and 1 teaspoon water; brush top of each baguette with egg mixture. Cover with greased plastic wrap. Let rise at room temperature (70°F to 80°F) until doubled in size, about 1 to 1½ hours.

5. Brush top of each baguette again with egg mixture. Bake at 450°F for 15 to 18 minutes or until deep golden brown. Remove from pans; cool on wire racks.

Basic White Bread

MAKES 2 LOAVES

½ cup low-fat (1%) milk

3 tablespoons sugar

2 teaspoons salt

3 tablespoons butter

2 packages active dry yeast

1½ cups warm water (105°F to 115°F)

5 to 6 cups all-purpose flour, divided

1. Place milk, sugar, salt and butter in small saucepan. Heat over low heat until butter melts and sugar dissolves. Cool to lukewarm.

2. Dissolve yeast in warm water in warmed bowl of electric stand mixer. Add lukewarm milk mixture and 4½ cups flour. Attach dough hook to mixer. Turn to low and mix 1 minute.

3. Continuing on low, add remaining flour, ½ cup at a time, and mix until dough clings to hook and cleans sides of bowl, about 2 minutes. Knead on low 2 minutes longer or until dough is smooth and elastic. Dough will be slightly sticky to the touch.

4. Place dough in greased bowl, turning to grease top. Cover; let rise in warm place, free from draft, about 1 hour or until doubled in bulk.

5. Punch dough down and divide in half. Shape each half into 1 loaf and place in greased 8½×4½×2½-inch loaf pan. Cover; let rise in warm place, free from draft, about 1 hour, or until doubled in bulk.

6. Bake at 400°F until golden brown, about 30 minutes. Remove from pans immediately and cool on wire racks.

Garlic Bread: Prepare dough, divide and roll out each half into 1 rectangle, as directed for Basic White Bread. Mix together ¼ cup softened butter and ⅛ teaspoon garlic powder in small bowl. Spread each rectangle with butter mixture. Finish rolling and shaping loaves. Place in well-greased 8½×4½×2½-inch loaf pans. Cover; let rise in warm place, free from draft, about 1 hour or until doubled in bulk. If desired, brush tops with additional melted butter and sprinkle of garlic powder. Bake at 375°F for 40 to 45 minutes or until golden brown. Remove from pans immediately and cool on wire racks.

Sixty-Minute Rolls: Increase yeast to 3 packages and sugar to ¼ cup. Mix and knead dough following steps 1 through 3. Place dough in greased bowl, turning to grease top. Cover; let rise in warm place, free from draft, about 15 minutes. Turn dough onto lightly floured surface. Shape as desired (see following suggestions). Cover. Let rise in slightly warm oven (90°F) about 15 minutes. Bake at 425°F for 12 minutes or until golden brown. Remove from pans immediately and cool on wire racks.

Curlicues: Divide dough in half and roll each half into 12×9-inch rectangle. Cut rectangle into 12 equal strips, about 1 inch wide. Roll each strip tightly to form a coil, tucking ends underneath. Place on greased baking sheets about 2 inches apart.

Cloverleafs: Divide dough into 24 equal pieces. Form each piece into a ball and place in greased muffin pan. With scissors, cut the top of each piece of dough first in half, then crosswise to make a cloverleaf pattern.

Garlic Pull-Apart Bread

MAKES 2 LOAVES

- **6 to 7 cups all-purpose flour, divided**
- **3 tablespoons sugar**
- **2 tablespoons garlic salt, divided**
- **2 packages active dry yeast**
- **1½ cups water**
- **½ cup milk**
- **½ cup (1 stick) butter, divided**

1. Place 5 cups flour, sugar, 1 tablespoon garlic salt and yeast in bowl of electric stand mixer. Attach dough hook to mixer. Turn to low and mix 15 seconds. Combine water, milk and ¼ cup butter in small saucepan. Heat over low heat until liquids are very warm (120°F to 130°F).

2. Turn mixer to low and gradually add warm liquids to flour mixture, about 30 seconds. Mix 1 minute longer. Continuing on low, add remaining flour, ½ cup at a time, until dough clings to hook and cleans sides of bowl. Knead on low 2 minutes longer.

3. Place in greased bowl, turning to grease top. Cover; let rise in warm place, free from draft, until doubled in bulk, about 1 hour.

4. Punch dough down and divide in half. Roll 1 half into 12×8×¼-inch rectangle. Melt remaining butter and mix with remaining garlic salt. Brush dough with mixture. Cut dough into 4 equal 8×3-inch strips. Stack strips and cut into 4 equal 3×2-inch strips. Place pieces on edge in greased 8½×4½×2½-inch loaf pan so strips form 1 row down length of pan. Repeat with remaining dough. Cover; let rise in warm place, free from draft, until doubled in bulk, about 1 hour. Bake at 400°F for 30 to 35 minutes. Remove from pans immediately; cool on wire racks.

Panettone

- 4 to 4½ cups all-purpose flour, divided
- 1 teaspoon salt
- ½ cup raisins
- 1 teaspoon grated lemon peel
- ½ cup chopped candied citron
- ¼ cup sugar
- 1 package active dry yeast
- 1 cup warm milk (105°F to 115°F)
- ½ cup vegetable oil
- ¼ cup (½ stick) butter, melted
- 4 egg yolks, beaten
- 1 egg white
- 1 tablespoon water

1. Place 3 cups flour, salt, raisins, lemon peel, candied citron and sugar in bowl of electric stand mixer. Attach dough hook to mixer. Turn to low and mix 15 seconds. Dissolve yeast in warm milk; add oil and butter.

2. Turn mixer to low. Gradually add warm milk mixture and egg yolks to flour mixture. Mix 1 minute. Continuing on low, add remaining flour, ½ cup at a time, until dough clings to hook* and cleans sides of bowl. Knead on low 2 minutes longer.

3. Place dough in greased bowl, turning to grease top. Cover; let rise in warm place, free from draft, until doubled in bulk, about 1 hour.

4. Punch dough down and shape into ball. Place in greased and floured 1½-quart soufflé dish. Let rise, uncovered, in warm place, free from draft, until doubled in bulk, about 1 hour.

5. Cut 2 slashes with sharp knife in cross pattern on top of loaf. Beat egg white and water together with fork. Brush top of loaf with mixture. Bake at 350°F for 55 to 60 minutes. Remove from baking dish immediately; cool on wire rack.

Dough may not form a ball on hook. However, as long as there is contact between dough and hook, kneading will be accomplished. Do not add more than the maximum amount of flour specified or a dry loaf will result.

Whole Grain Wheat Bread

MAKES 2 LOAVES

- ⅓ cup plus 1 tablespoon packed brown sugar, divided
- 2 cups warm water (105°F to 115°F)
- 2 packages active dry yeast
- 5 to 6 cups whole wheat flour, divided
- ¾ cup powdered milk
- 2 teaspoons salt
- ⅓ cup oil

1. Dissolve 1 tablespoon brown sugar in warm water in small bowl. Add yeast and let mixture stand.

2. Place 4 cups flour, powdered milk, ⅓ cup brown sugar and salt in bowl of electric stand mixer. Attach dough hook to mixer. Turn to low and mix 15 seconds. Continuing on low, gradually add yeast mixture and oil to flour mixture and mix 1½ minutes longer. Stop and scrape bowl.

3. Continuing on low, add remaining flour, ½ cup at a time, and mix until dough clings to hook* and cleans sides of bowl, about 2 minutes. Knead on low about 2 minutes longer.

4. Place dough in greased bowl, turning to grease top. Cover; let rise in warm place, free from draft, about 1 hour or until doubled in bulk. Punch dough down and divide in half. Shape each half into loaf. Place in greased 8½×4½×2½-inch loaf pan. Cover; let rise in warm place, free from draft, about 1 hour or until doubled in bulk.

5. Bake at 400°F for 15 minutes. Reduce oven temperature to 350°F and bake 30 minutes longer. Remove from pans immediately; cool on wire racks.

*Dough may not form a ball on hook. However, as long as hook comes in contact with dough, kneading will be accomplished. Do not add more than the maximum amount of flour specified or a dry loaf will result.

Three-Grain Bread

1 **cup whole wheat flour**

¾ **cup all-purpose flour**

1 **package rapid-rise active dry yeast**

1 **cup milk**

2 **tablespoons honey**

3 **teaspoons olive oil**

1 **teaspoon salt**

½ **cup old-fashioned oats, plus extra for topping (optional)**

¼ **cup whole-grain cornmeal**

1 **egg beaten with 1 tablespoon water (optional)**

1. Preheat oven to 375°F. Combine whole wheat flour, all-purpose flour and yeast in bowl of electric stand mixer. Stir milk, honey, olive oil and salt in small saucepan over low heat until warm (120°F to 140°F). Stir milk mixture into flour mixture. Turn mixer to high and beat 3 minutes. Reduce speed to low. Mix in oats and cornmeal. If dough is too wet, add additional flour by teaspoonfuls until it begins to come together.

2. Attach dough hook to mixer. Knead on low until dough clings to hook and cleans sides of bowl. Turn mixer to medium and knead 5 minutes more. Place dough in large, lightly oiled bowl; turn once to oil surface. Cover; let rise in warm place, free from draft, about 1 hour or until dough is puffy and does not spring back when touched.

3. Punch dough down and shape into 1 (8-inch-long) loaf. Place on baking sheet lightly dusted with cornmeal or flour. Cover; let rise in warm place until almost doubled in bulk, about 45 minutes.

4. Make shallow slash down center of loaf with sharp knife. Brush lightly with egg mixture and sprinkle with oats, if desired. Bake 30 minutes or until loaf sounds hollow when tapped. Remove to wire rack to cool.

French Bread

MAKES 2 LOAVES

2 packages active dry yeast

2½ cups warm water (105°F to 115°F)

1 tablespoon salt

1 tablespoon butter, melted

7 cups all-purpose flour

2 tablespoons cornmeal

1 egg white

1 tablespoon cold water

1. Dissolve yeast in warm water in warmed bowl of electric stand mixer. Add salt, butter and flour. Attach dough hook to mixer. Turn to low and mix until well blended, about 1 minute. Knead on low about 2 minutes longer. Dough will be sticky.

2. Place dough in greased bowl, turning to grease top. Cover; let rise in warm place, free from draft, about 1 hour or until doubled in bulk.

3. Punch dough down and divide in half. Roll each half into 12×15-inch rectangle. Roll dough tightly, from longest side, tapering ends if desired. Place loaves on greased baking sheets that have been dusted with cornmeal. Cover; let rise in warm place, free from draft, about 1 hour or until doubled in bulk.

4. With sharp knife, make 4 diagonal cuts on top of each loaf. Bake at 450°F for 25 minutes. Remove from oven. Beat egg white and cold water together with fork. Brush each loaf with egg mixture. Return to oven and bake 5 minutes longer. Remove from baking sheets immediately; cool on wire racks.

Light Rye Bread

MAKES 2 LOAVES

¼ **cup honey**

¼ **cup light molasses**

2 **teaspoons salt**

2 **tablespoons butter**

2 **tablespoons caraway seeds**

1 **cup boiling water**

2 **packages active dry yeast**

¾ **cup warm water (105°F to 115°F)**

2 **cups rye flour**

3¼ **to 4 cups all-purpose flour, divided**

1. Place honey, molasses, salt, butter, caraway seeds and boiling water in small bowl. Stir until honey dissolves. Cool to lukewarm.

2. Dissolve yeast in warm water in warmed bowl of electric stand mixer. Add lukewarm honey mixture, rye flour and 1 cup all-purpose flour. Attach dough hook to mixer. Turn to low and mix until well mixed, about 1 minute. Stop and scrape bowl if necessary.

3. Continuing on low, add remaining all-purpose flour, ½ cup at a time, and mix about 2 minutes or until dough clings to hook and cleans sides of bowl. Knead on low about 2 minutes longer.

4. Place dough in greased bowl, turning to grease top. Cover; let rise in warm place, free from draft, about 1 hour or until doubled in bulk.

5. Punch dough down and divide in half. Shape each half into round loaf. Place on 2 greased baking sheets. Cover; let rise in warm place, free from draft, 45 to 60 minutes or until doubled in bulk.

6. Bake at 350°F for 30 to 45 minutes. Cover loaves with aluminum foil for last 15 minutes if tops brown too quickly. Remove from baking sheets immediately; cool on wire racks.

Rapid Mix Cool Rise White Bread

MAKES 2 LOAVES

- 6 **to 7 cups all-purpose flour, divided**
- 2 **tablespoons sugar**
- 3½ **teaspoons salt**
- 3 **packages active dry yeast**
- ¼ **cup butter, softened**
- 2 **cups very warm water (120°F to 130°F)**

1. Place 5½ cups flour, sugar, salt, yeast and butter in bowl of electric stand mixer. Attach dough hook to mixer. Turn to low and mix 20 seconds. Gradually add warm water and mix 1½ minutes longer.

2. Continuing on low, add remaining flour, ½ cup at a time, and mix until dough clings to hook* and cleans sides of bowl, about 2 minutes. Knead on low about 2 minutes longer.

3. Cover dough with plastic wrap and a towel. Let rest 20 minutes.

4. Divide dough in half. Shape each half into 1 loaf. Place loaves in greased 8½×4½×2½-inch loaf pans. Brush each loaf with oil and cover loosely with plastic wrap. Refrigerate 2 to 12 hours.

5. When ready to bake, uncover dough carefully. Let stand at room temperature 10 minutes. Puncture gas bubbles that may have formed. Bake at 400°F for 35 to 40 minutes. Remove from pans immediately and cool on wire racks.

Dough may not form a ball on hook. However, as long as hook comes in contact with dough, kneading will be accomplished. Do not add more than the maximum amount of flour specified or a dry loaf will result.

Bourbon Street Beignets

MAKES 60 BEIGNETS

1 package active dry yeast

¼ cup warm water (105°F to 115°F)

¼ cup granulated sugar

2 tablespoons shortening

½ teaspoon salt

½ cup boiling water

½ cup heavy cream

1 egg, beaten

4 to 4½ cups all-purpose flour

Oil for deep frying

Powdered sugar

tip

Doughnuts can be filled with custard, whipped cream, or jelly using a small pastry tube.

1. Dissolve yeast in warm water; set aside. Place granulated sugar, shortening, salt and boiling water in bowl of electric stand mixer. Stir until shortening is melted and sugar dissolves; cool to lukewarm. Add cream, egg, 3 cups flour and yeast. Attach dough hook to mixer. Turn to low and mix 2 minutes. Add remaining flour, ½ cup at a time, until dough clings to hook and cleans sides of bowl, about 2 minutes. Knead on low 2 minutes longer.

2. Place dough on lightly floured board and roll into 10×24-inch rectangle. Using sharp knife, cut dough into 2-inch squares.

3. Pour oil into large heavy saucepan or deep fryer to depth of 2 inches. Heat oil to 360°F. Fry doughnuts, 4 at a time, turning to brown on both sides, about 3 minutes. Drain on paper towels and sprinkle with powdered sugar.

Pepperoni Cheese Bread

1. Preheat oven to 350°F. Dissolve yeast in warm beer and milk in bowl of electric stand mixer. Attach dough hook to mixer. Turn to low speed and add rye flour, basil, sugar, salt, red pepper flakes and 2 cups all-purpose flour. Mix until smooth. Add enough remaining all-purpose flour to form stiff dough.

2. Add cheese and pepperoni. Knead 2 to 3 minutes or until smooth and elastic. Transfer to greased bowl, turning once to grease top. Cover; let rise, uncovered, in warm place, free from draft, until doubled in bulk, about 1 hour.

3. Punch dough down; divide in half. Shape into 2 (12-inch-long) loaves. Place on greased baking sheets. Cover; let rise in warm place until doubled again, about 45 minutes. Bake bread 30 to 35 minutes or until golden brown. Remove from oven and brush with oil. Serve warm or cool.

MAKES 2 LOAVES

- 1 package active dry yeast
- 1 cup warm beer (105°F to 115°F)
- ½ cup warm milk (105°F to 115°F)
- 1 cup rye flour
- 1 tablespoon dried basil
- 1 teaspoon sugar
- 1 teaspoon salt
- 1 teaspoon red pepper flakes
- 2¼ cups all-purpose flour, divided
- 1 cup shredded sharp Cheddar cheese
- 1 cup finely chopped pepperoni
- 1 tablespoon olive oil

tip

Serve bread with oregano-infused dipping oil. Combine 2 tablespoons olive oil, ½ teaspoon black pepper, 1 tablespoon chopped green olives, and 1 sprig fresh oregano. Let sit several hours before serving to blend flavors.

English Muffins

MAKES 32 MUFFINS

1½ teaspoons active dry yeast

¼ cup warm water (105°F to 115°F)

2½ cups plus 2 tablespoons all-purpose flour

1¼ teaspoons salt

¾ cup milk

1 tablespoon honey

3 tablespoons melted butter

Cornmeal

1. Dissolve yeast in warm water in small bowl; set aside. Mix flour and salt in bowl of electric stand mixer.

2. Combine yeast mixture with milk, honey and melted butter. Pour wet ingredients over dry ingredients in mixer bowl. Attach dough hook to mixer. Turn mixer to low. Mix 2 to 3 minutes or until dough separates from sides of bowl and forms a ball. Knead 2 minutes more.

3. Place dough in lightly oiled bowl. Cover with plastic wrap and let rest in warm place, free from draft, 1 to 1½ hours or until dough is doubled in bulk.

4. Transfer dough to lightly floured surface. Roll dough into ½-inch-thick circle. Using biscuit cutter or drinking glass rim, cut dough into 3-inch circles, re-rolling if necessary.

5. Place dough pieces on baking sheet. Cover loosely with plastic wrap and let rise 30 minutes.

6. Dust cast-iron skillet with cornmeal and heat over medium-low heat. Place 4 dough circles in skillet and cook 5 to 8 minutes on each side. Transfer muffins from skillet to oven. Bake at 350°F for 6 minutes. Repeat with remaining dough. Cool 10 to 15 minutes. Split with fork to serve.

Popovers

1. Place eggs, milk, butter, flour and salt in bowl of electric stand mixer. Attach wire whip to mixer. Turn to medium-low and beat 15 seconds. Stop and scrape bowl. Turn to medium-low and beat 15 seconds more.

2. Fill 8 heavily greased and floured custard cups half full with batter. Place cups on cookie sheet. Place cookie sheet in cold oven and set heat at 450°F. Bake 15 minutes; reduce heat to 350°F and bake 20 to 25 minutes longer. Remove from oven and cut slit into side of each popover. Serve immediately.

MAKES 8 POPOVERS

2	eggs
1	cup milk
1	tablespoon butter, melted
1	cup all-purpose flour
¼	teaspoon salt

Brioche Ring

MAKES 2 LOAVES

- 2 **packages active dry yeast**
- 1 **cup warm milk (105°F to 115°F)**
- 3¾ **to 4¼ cups unbleached all-purpose flour, divided**
- ¾ **cup (1½ sticks) butter, softened**
- 9 **tablespoons sugar, divided**
- 1 **teaspoon salt**
- 3 **eggs**
- 2 **egg yolks, divided**
- 2 **tablespoons milk**
- 3 **tablespoons chopped pecans**

Sponge

1. Dissolve yeast in warm milk in medium bowl. Add 1¾ cups flour and mix thoroughly. Cover bowl with plastic wrap and allow mixture to rise 45 minutes.

Dough

2. Place butter, 6 tablespoons sugar and salt in bowl of electric stand mixer. Attach flat beater to mixer. Turn to medium-low and cream ingredients 1 minute. Stop and scrape bowl. Turn to low and add eggs and 1 egg yolk, 1 at a time, beating 15 seconds after each addition.

3. Exchange beater for dough hook and add 1¾ cups flour. Turn to low and mix 1 minute until well combined. Continuing on low, add remaining flour, ¼ cup at a time, until dough clings to hook and cleans sides of bowl.

4. Add sponge to dough. Turn to low and knead 3 minutes. Sponge should knead into dough completely within 3 minutes.

5. Place dough in greased bowl, turning to grease top. Cover; let rise at room temperature, until doubled in bulk, about 2 hours. Punch dough down. Cover bowl with plastic wrap and refrigerate at least 4 hours or overnight.

6. Punch dough down and divide in half. Shape 1 half into ball. Poke hole through center of ball and gently widen by stretching dough. Continue stretching to make doughnut-shaped ring 8 to 9 inches in diameter. Place ring on greased baking sheet. Place 1½-pint bowl, the outside of which has been well greased, upside down in center of ring to prevent hole from closing during baking. Repeat with remaining dough. Cover; let rise in warm place, free from draft, until doubled in bulk, about 1 hour.

7. Beat remaining egg yolk and milk together. Brush mixture on each ring. Sprinkle dough with chopped pecans and remaining 3 tablespoons sugar. Bake at 350°F for 30 to 35 minutes. Remove from baking sheets immediately and cool on wire racks.

Crusty Pizza Dough

1. Dissolve yeast in warm water in warmed bowl of electric stand mixer. Add salt, olive oil and 2½ cups flour. Attach dough hook to mixer. Turn to low and mix 1 minute.

2. Continuing on low, add remaining flour, ½ cup at a time, and mix until dough clings to hook and cleans sides of bowl, about 2 minutes. Knead on low about 2 minutes longer.

3. Place dough in greased bowl, turning to grease top. Cover; let rise in warm place, free from draft, about 1 hour, or until doubled in bulk. Punch dough down.

4. Brush 14-inch pizza pan with oil. Sprinkle with cornmeal. Press dough across bottom of pan, forming collar around edge to hold toppings. Add toppings as desired. Bake at 450°F for 15 to 20 minutes.

MAKES 4 SERVINGS

- 1 **package active dry yeast**
- 1 **cup warm water (105°F to 115°F)**
- ½ **teaspoon salt**
- 2 **teaspoons olive oil**
- 2½ **to 3½ cups all-purpose flour, divided**
- 1 **tablespoon cornmeal**

Chili Corn Bread

Nonstick cooking spray

¼ cup chopped red bell pepper

¼ cup chopped green bell pepper

2 small jalapeño peppers,* minced

2 cloves garlic, minced

¾ cup corn

1½ cups yellow cornmeal

½ cup all-purpose flour

2 tablespoons sugar

2 teaspoons baking powder

½ teaspoon baking soda

½ teaspoon ground cumin

½ teaspoon salt

1½ cups low-fat buttermilk

2 egg whites

1 egg

4 tablespoons (½ stick) butter, melted

Jalapeño peppers can sting and irritate the skin, so wear rubber gloves when handling peppers and do not touch your eyes.

1. Preheat oven to 425°F. Spray 8-inch square baking pan with nonstick cooking spray; set aside.

2. Spray small skillet with cooking spray. Add bell peppers, jalapeño peppers and garlic; cook and stir 3 to 4 minutes or until peppers are tender. Stir in corn; cook 1 to 2 minutes. Remove from heat.

3. Combine cornmeal, flour, sugar, baking powder, baking soda, cumin and salt in bowl of electric stand mixer. Add buttermilk, egg whites, egg and butter; mix at low speed until blended. Stir in corn mixture. Pour batter into prepared baking pan.

4. Bake 25 to 30 minutes or until golden brown. Cool on wire rack. Cut into 12 squares before serving.

Walnut Fig Bread

1. Preheat oven to 350°F. Combine 1 cup all-purpose flour, whole wheat flour, yeast, fennel seeds and salt in bowl of electric stand mixer. In small saucepan, combine beer, butter and honey; heat to 120°F. Add beer mixture to dry ingredients. Turn mixer to low. Stir until moistened. Add egg and beat until smooth. Add enough remaining all-purpose flour to form a soft dough (dough will be slightly sticky). Stir in figs and walnuts.

2. Attach dough hook to mixer. Knead on low until dough clings to hook and cleans sides of bowl. Turn mixer to medium and knead 5 minutes more. Transfer dough to greased bowl, turning once to grease top. Cover and let rise in warm place until doubled in bulk, about 1 hour.

3. Punch dough down. Shape into round loaf and place on greased baking sheet. Cover and let rise in warm place 40 minutes. Bake 30 to 35 minutes or until browned. Cool on wire rack. Serve with cream cheese.

MAKES 1 LOAF

2¼ cups all-purpose flour, divided

1 cup whole wheat flour

1 package active dry yeast

1 tablespoon whole fennel seeds

1½ teaspoons salt

1 cup honey beer

2 tablespoons butter

1 tablespoon honey

1 egg

1 cup chopped dried figs

½ cup chopped walnuts, toasted

Softened cream cheese (optional)

Cakes, Cupcakes, and Frostings

Discover confectionery bliss in sweets of all shapes and sizes

Molten Cinnamon-Chocolate Cupcakes

MAKES 6 CUPCAKES

- 6 ounces semisweet baking chocolate
- ¾ cup (1½ sticks) butter
- 1½ cups powdered sugar, plus extra for garnish
- 4 eggs
- 6 tablespoons all-purpose flour
- ¾ teaspoon ground cinnamon
- 1½ teaspoons vanilla

1. Preheat oven to 425°F. Spray 6 jumbo muffin cups or 6 (1-cup) custard cups with nonstick cooking spray.

2. Combine chocolate and butter in medium microwaveable bowl; heat on HIGH 1½ minutes, stirring every 30 seconds, until melted and smooth. Place in bowl of electric stand mixer. Add powdered sugar, eggs, flour, cinnamon and vanilla; beat at medium speed until well blended. Pour batter into prepared muffin cups, filling slightly more than half full.

3. Bake 13 minutes or until cupcakes spring back when lightly touched but centers are soft. Let stand 1 minute; loosen sides with knife. Gently lift out cupcakes and invert onto serving plate; sprinkle with powdered sugar. Serve immediately.

Velvety Coconut and Spice Cake

MAKES 1 CAKE

½ cup granulated sugar plus additional for preparing cake pans

2½ cups all-purpose flour

1½ teaspoons baking powder

¾ teaspoon baking soda

½ teaspoon salt

1½ teaspoons ground cinnamon

¼ teaspoon ground cloves

¼ teaspoon ground nutmeg

¼ teaspoon ground allspice

¼ teaspoon ground cardamom

½ cup (1 stick) butter, softened

½ cup packed brown sugar

4 eggs

1 teaspoon vanilla

1½ cups light cream

¼ cup molasses

1½ cups shredded coconut

Creamy Orange Frosting (recipe follows)

Candied Orange Rose (recipe follows, optional)

⅔ cup orange marmalade

1. Preheat oven to 350°F. Grease 3 (8-inch) round cake pans; sprinkle with enough granulated sugar to lightly coat bottoms and sides of pans.

2. Combine flour, baking powder, baking soda, salt and spices in medium bowl; set aside.

3. Beat butter in bowl of electric stand mixer at medium speed until creamy. Add ½ cup granulated sugar and brown sugar; beat until light and fluffy. Add eggs, 1 at a time, beating well after each addition. Blend in vanilla.

4. Combine cream and molasses in small bowl. Add flour mixture to egg mixture alternately with molasses mixture, beating well after each addition. Stir in coconut; pour evenly into prepared pans.

5. Bake 20 minutes or until toothpicks inserted into centers come out clean. Cool in pans on wire racks 10 minutes. Loosen edges; remove to racks to cool completely.

6. Prepare Creamy Orange Frosting and Candied Orange Rose, if desired.

7. To assemble, spread 2 cake layers with marmalade; stack on serving plate. Top with third cake layer. Frost with Creamy Orange Frosting. Refrigerate. Garnish with Candied Orange Rose, if desired.

Creamy Orange Frosting

1 package (3 ounces) cream cheese, softened

2 cups powdered sugar

Few drops orange extract

Milk (optional)

1. Beat cream cheese in bowl of electric stand mixer at medium speed until creamy. Gradually add powdered sugar, beating until fluffy. Blend in orange extract.

2. If necessary, add milk, 1 teaspoonful at a time, for a thinner consistency.

Candied Orange Rose

1. Combine 1 cup granulated sugar and 1 cup water in medium saucepan. Bring to a boil over medium-high heat, stirring occasionally.

2. Meanwhile, thinly peel 1 orange with sharp knife, leaving as much membrane on orange as possible.

3. Carefully roll up peel, starting at one short end; secure with toothpick.

4. Place on slotted spoon; add to hot sugar syrup.

5. Reduce heat to low; simmer 5 to 10 minutes or until orange rind turns translucent. Remove from syrup; place on waxed paper-covered cookie sheet to cool. Remove toothpick.

tip

For an alternate garnish, consider topping your cake with a sprinkle of grated orange peel, ground cinnamon, or sweetened flaked coconut.

Almond Raspberry Cream Cupcakes

MAKES 18 CUPCAKES

2¾ cups all-purpose flour

2½ teaspoons baking powder

¾ teaspoon salt

1¾ cups granulated sugar

¾ cup (1½ sticks) butter, softened

1 teaspoon almond extract

1 teaspoon vanilla

4 eggs

2 egg yolks

1½ cups milk

Raspberry Cream (recipe follows)

Powdered sugar

1. Preheat oven to 350°F. Line 18 standard (2½-inch) muffin cups with paper baking cups.

2. Combine flour, baking powder and salt in medium bowl; set aside. Beat sugar, butter, almond extract and vanilla in bowl of electric stand mixer at medium speed 4 minutes or until light and fluffy. Add eggs and egg yolks, 1 at a time, beating well after each addition. Alternately add flour mixture and milk, beating well after each addition. Spoon batter into prepared muffin cups, filling three-fourths full.

3. Bake 20 to 22 minutes or until toothpick inserted into centers comes out clean. Cool cupcakes in pans 15 minutes. Remove from pans; cool completely on wire racks.

4. Prepare Raspberry Cream. Cut tops off cupcakes; spread with Raspberry Cream. Replace cupcake tops; sprinkle with powdered sugar.

Raspberry Cream: Beat 1 cup cold whipping cream and ¼ cup powdered sugar in bowl of electric stand mixer at high speed 5 minutes or until cream is thickened and almost stiff. Place 1 pint fresh raspberries in small bowl; mash lightly with fork. Gently fold raspberries into whipped cream mixture until well blended and evenly colored.

Caramel Walnut Banana Torte

MAKES 1 TORTE

- 1 cup firmly packed brown sugar
- 1 cup (2 sticks) butter, softened, divided
- ½ cup whipping cream
- 1 cup chopped walnuts
- 1½ cups granulated sugar
- 1 cup mashed ripe banana (about 2 medium bananas)
- 1 teaspoon vanilla
- 3 eggs
- 2½ cups all-purpose flour
- 1¼ teaspoons baking powder
- 1 teaspoon baking soda
- ½ teaspoon salt
- ¾ cup buttermilk
  Banana Filling (recipe follows)
- 2 medium bananas, thinly sliced, divided
- ½ cup whipping cream, whipped

1. Place brown sugar, ½ cup butter and cream in small saucepan. Cook over low heat, stirring constantly, until butter melts. Divide among 3 (8- to 9-inch) round cake pans, turning to evenly coat bottom. Divide walnuts among pans; set pans aside.

2. Place granulated sugar and remaining ½ cup butter in bowl of electric stand mixer. Attach flat beater to mixer. Turn to low and mix about 30 seconds. Stop and scrape bowl. Add mashed bananas and vanilla. Mix about 30 seconds. Continuing on low, add eggs, 1 at a time, mixing about 15 seconds after each addition. Stop and scrape bowl.

3. Combine flour, baking powder, baking soda and salt in medium bowl. Add half of flour mixture to sugar mixture in mixer bowl. Turn to low and mix about 30 seconds. Add buttermilk and remaining flour mixture. Gradually turn to medium and beat 30 seconds. Spread batter evenly over topping in pans. Bake at 350°F for 25 to 30 minutes or until toothpick inserted in centers comes out clean. Cool in pans about 3 minutes. Invert onto wire racks and cool completely.

4. Place 1 cake layer, walnut side up, on large plate. Spread with half of Banana Filling. Arrange half of banana slices over Banana Filling. Top with second layer, walnut side up. Spread with remaining filling and banana slices. Top with remaining cake layer, walnut side up. Top torte with whipped cream. Store in refrigerator.

Banana Filling

- ½ cup sugar
- 3 tablespoons all-purpose flour
- ¼ teaspoon salt
- 1 cup low-fat (1%) milk
- 1 egg, beaten
- 1 teaspoon vanilla
- 1 tablespoon butter

Combine sugar, flour and salt in medium saucepan. Gradually stir in milk. Bring to a boil over medium heat, stirring constantly. Stir about ¼ cup hot mixture into beaten egg in separate bowl. (Add hot mixture slowly so eggs do not scramble.) Pour egg mixture into saucepan. Cook until mixture is bubbly, stirring constantly. Remove from heat. Stir in vanilla and butter. Cool slightly. Refrigerate 1 hour while cake cools.

Chocolate Roll

4 eggs, separated

¾ cup granulated sugar, divided

½ teaspoon vanilla

¾ cup cake flour

1 teaspoon baking powder

¼ teaspoon salt

¼ cup cocoa

Powdered sugar

Whipped Cream Filling (recipe follows)

1. Place egg yolks in bowl of electric stand mixer. Attach wire whip to mixer. Turn to high and whip until light and lemon colored, about 2 minutes. Continuing at high speed, gradually sprinkle in ¼ cup sugar and vanilla; beat 2 minutes more. Remove from bowl and set aside.

2. Place egg whites in clean mixer bowl. Attach wire whip to mixer. Turn to high and whip until whites begin to hold shape. Continuing at high speed, gradually sprinkle in remaining ½ cup sugar, whipping until stiff but not dry.

3. Fold egg yolk mixture into egg whites. Sift flour, baking powder, salt and cocoa together. Fold into egg mixture.

4. Line 10½×15½×1-inch jelly roll pan with waxed paper and grease. Pour batter into pan and bake at 375°F for 10 to 12 minutes. Remove from oven and immediately turn onto paper towel sprinkled with powdered sugar. Remove waxed paper, and roll cake and towel together; cool completely.

5. When cool, unroll cake and spread with Whipped Cream Filling. Reroll and sprinkle with powdered sugar.

Whipped Cream Filling

1 cup heavy cream

½ teaspoon vanilla

3 tablespoons sugar

Place cream and vanilla in bowl of electric stand mixer. Attach wire whip to mixer. Turn to high and whip until cream begins to thicken. Continuing at high speed, gradually sprinkle in sugar, whipping until stiff.

Makes about 1 cup

Cranberry Pound Cake

MAKES 12 SERVINGS

- 1 cup (2 sticks) unsalted butter
- 1½ cups sugar
- ¼ teaspoon salt
- ¼ teaspoon ground mace
- 4 eggs
- 2 cups cake flour
- 1 cup chopped fresh or frozen cranberries

tip

Mace is a delicate spice similar in flavor to nutmeg because it is the thin bright red layer that encompasses the nutmeg shell. Mace can be found in the spice aisle in most major grocery stores.

1. Preheat oven to 350°F. Grease and flour 9×5-inch loaf pan.

2. Beat butter, sugar, salt and mace in bowl of electric stand mixer at medium speed until light and fluffy. Beat in eggs, 1 at a time, until well blended. Reduce speed to low; add flour, ½ cup at a time, scraping down bowl occasionally. Fold in cranberries.

3. Spoon batter into prepared pan. Bake 60 to 70 minutes or until toothpick inserted into center comes out clean. Cool in pan on wire rack 5 minutes. Run knife around edges of pan to loosen cake; cool additional 30 minutes in pan. Remove from pan; cool completely on wire rack.

Mini Sweetheart Chocolate Cakes

MAKES 6 MINI CAKES

1⅔ cups all-purpose flour

½ cup unsweetened cocoa powder

1 teaspoon baking soda

¼ teaspoon salt

1 cup plus 2 tablespoons buttermilk

¾ cup mayonnaise

¾ cup packed brown sugar

1 teaspoon vanilla

1 cup semisweet chocolate chips, divided

¼ cup whipping cream

1. Preheat oven to 350°F. Spray 6 mini tube pans or cake pans with nonstick cooking spray; set aside.

2. Combine flour, cocoa, baking soda and salt in medium bowl. Beat buttermilk, mayonnaise, brown sugar and vanilla in bowl of electric stand mixer at medium speed until well blended. Gradually add flour mixture; beat 2 minutes or until well blended. Stir in ½ cup chocolate chips.

3. Spoon batter evenly into prepared pans. Bake 22 minutes or until toothpick inserted near centers comes out clean. Cool cakes in pans 15 minutes; invert onto wire rack to cool completely.

4. Place remaining chocolate chips in small bowl. Heat cream in small saucepan over low heat until bubbles form around edge of pan; pour over chips. Let stand 5 minutes; stir until smooth. Cool until slightly thickened; drizzle over cakes.

Easy White Cake

MAKES 1 CAKE

2 cups all-purpose flour
1½ cups sugar
3 teaspoons baking powder
½ teaspoon salt
½ cup shortening
1 cup low-fat (1%) milk
1 teaspoon vanilla
4 egg whites

1. Combine dry ingredients in bowl of electric stand mixer. Add shortening, milk and vanilla. Attach flat beater to mixer. Turn to low and mix about 1 minute. Stop and scrape bowl. Add egg whites. Turn to medium and beat about 1 minute or until smooth and fluffy.

2. Pour batter into 2 greased and floured 8- or 9-inch round baking pans. Bake at 350°F for 30 to 35 minutes or until toothpick inserted in center comes out clean. Cool 10 minutes. Remove from pans. Cool completely on wire rack. Frost, if desired.

Fluffy Frosting

MAKES 2 CUPS

1½ cups sugar
½ cup water
1½ tablespoons light corn syrup
½ teaspoon cream of tartar
½ teaspoon salt
2 egg whites
1½ teaspoons vanilla

1. Place sugar, water, corn syrup, cream of tartar and salt in saucepan. Cook and stir over medium heat until sugar is completely dissolved, forming a syrup.

2. Place egg whites and vanilla in bowl of electric stand mixer. Attach wire whip to mixer. Turn to high and whip about 45 seconds or until egg whites begin to hold shape. Continuing at high speed, slowly pour hot syrup into egg whites in a fine stream. Whip about 5 minutes longer or until frosting loses its gloss and stands in stiff peaks. Frost cake immediately.

Fluffy Chocolate Frosting: Melt 3 squares (1 ounce each) unsweetened chocolate with sugar, water, corn syrup, cream of tartar and salt. Proceed as directed above.

Fluffy Peppermint Frosting: Omit vanilla and add 1 teaspoon peppermint extract and ¼ cup crushed peppermint candy. Proceed as directed above.

Fluffy Amaretto Frosting: Omit vanilla and add 2½ teaspoons Amaretto liqueur. Proceed as directed above.

Fluffy Lemon Frosting: Omit vanilla and add 1 teaspoon lemon extract and 2 teaspoons grated lemon peel. Proceed as directed above.

Light-N-Luscious Lemon Pavé

MAKES 10 SERVINGS

- 4 **eggs, separated**
- ¾ **cup granulated sugar**
- ½ **tablespoon vegetable oil**
- 1 **teaspoon vanilla**
- ¾ **cup cake flour**
- 1 **teaspoon baking powder**
- ½ **teaspoon salt**
  Powdered sugar
  Lemon Filling (recipe follows)
  Lemon Buttercream Frosting (recipe follows)

1. Place egg whites in bowl of electric stand mixer. Attach wire whip to mixer. Turn to high and whip until stiff but not dry. Remove from bowl and set aside.

2. Place egg yolks and granulated sugar in mixer bowl. Turn to medium and whip until thick and lemon colored, about 1 minute. Stop and scrape bowl. Add oil and vanilla. Turn to medium-low and whip 30 seconds. Gently fold egg whites into egg yolk mixture.

3. Sift flour, baking powder and salt together. Fold half of flour mixture into egg mixture. Repeat with remaining flour mixture.

4. Pour batter into 10×15×1-inch jelly roll pan that has been lined with waxed paper, greased and floured. Bake at 375°F for 10 to 12 minutes. Immediately loosen cake from pan and invert onto towel sprinkled with powdered sugar; cool completely.

5. Cut cake crosswise to form 3 (5×10×1-inch) layers. Spread Lemon Filling between layers. Cover cake tightly with plastic wrap and refrigerate at least 4 hours. Frost and decorate with Lemon Buttercream Frosting.

Lemon Filling: Combine 5 egg yolks, ⅓ cup granulated sugar and ½ cup lemon juice in double boiler over boiling water. Cook, stirring constantly, until mixture is very thick, about 5 minutes; do not boil. Remove from heat. Add 4 tablespoons butter, 1 tablespoon at a time, beating until thoroughly incorporated. Stir in 1 teaspoon grated lemon peel. Cover mixture and refrigerate 1 hour. Place ½ cup heavy cream in mixer bowl. Attach wire whip to mixer. Turn to high and whip until stiff. Fold whipped cream into egg mixture. Refrigerate until ready to use.

Lemon Buttercream Frosting: Place 1¼ cups softened butter, 2 teaspoons grated lemon peel and 3 tablespoons lemon juice in bowl of electric stand mixer. Attach flat beater to mixer. Turn to medium and beat 30 seconds. Stop and scrape bowl. Sift 3 cups powdered sugar into bowl. Turn to low and beat 30 seconds. Stop and scrape bowl. Turn to medium and beat until fluffy, about 2 minutes.

Plum Pudding Cake

¾ **cup sugar, divided**

¼ **cup all-purpose flour**

¼ **teaspoon salt**

¼ **teaspoon ground cinnamon**

3 **tablespoons melted unsalted butter**

Grated peel of 1 lemon

1 **tablespoon lemon juice**

3 **large eggs, separated**

1½ **cups milk**

1½ **cups finely chopped plums, unpeeled (about 4 plums)**

Cherry-vanilla ice cream (optional)

1. Preheat oven to 350°F. Lightly coat 8 miniature round baking pans with nonstick cooking spray.

2. Combine ½ cup plus 1 tablespoon sugar, flour, salt and cinnamon in large bowl. Add melted butter, lemon peel and lemon juice. Beat 3 egg yolks with milk in small bowl. Stir into flour mixture; set aside.

3. Place egg whites in bowl of electric stand mixer. Attach wire whip; beat at medium speed until soft peaks form. Beat in remaining 3 tablespoons sugar; continue beating until stiff peaks form. Gently fold into flour mixture until well blended.

4. Pour batter into prepared baking pans. Sprinkle on chopped plums. Bake in water bath (place pans in 13✕9-inch baking dish; fill larger pan with 1 inch hot water). Bake 35 to 40 minutes or until cakes puff up and are firm to the touch. Remove from oven; cool 10 minutes. Serve plain or with cherry-vanilla ice cream.

Strawberry Short Cupcake

MAKES 18 CUPCAKES

- 2 cups all-purpose flour
- 2½ teaspoons baking powder
- ½ teaspoon salt
- 1 cup milk
- 1 teaspoon vanilla
- 1½ cups plus 3 tablespoons sugar, divided
- ½ cup (1 stick) butter, softened
- 3 eggs
- 1½ cups cold whipping cream
- 2 quarts fresh strawberries, sliced

1. Preheat oven to 350°F. Spray 18 standard (2½-inch) muffin cups with nonstick cooking spray.

2. Combine flour, baking powder and salt in medium bowl. Combine milk and vanilla in measuring cup. Place 1½ cups sugar and butter in bowl of electric stand mixer. Beat at medium speed about 3 minutes or until creamy. Add eggs, 1 at a time, beating well after each addition. Add flour mixture alternately with milk mixture, beating until well blended. Spoon batter into prepared muffin cups, filling about three-fourths full.

3. Bake 18 to 20 minutes or until toothpick inserted into centers comes out clean. Cool cupcakes in pans 10 minutes. Remove from pans; cool completely on wire racks.

4. Beat cream in bowl of electric stand mixer at high speed until soft peaks form. Gradually add remaining 3 tablespoons sugar; beat until stiff peaks form.

5. Cut cupcakes in half crosswise. Top each bottom half with about 2 tablespoons whipped cream and strawberries. Top with top half of cupcake, whipped cream and additional strawberries.

Quick Yellow Cake

MAKES 1 CAKE

2¼ cups all-purpose flour

1½ cups sugar

3 teaspoons baking powder

½ teaspoon salt

½ cup shortening

1 cup low-fat (1%) milk

1 teaspoon vanilla

2 eggs

1. Combine dry ingredients in bowl of electric stand mixer. Add shortening, milk and vanilla. Attach flat beater to mixer. Turn to low and mix about 1 minute. Stop and scrape bowl. Add eggs. Continuing at low speed, mix about 30 seconds. Stop and scrape bowl. Turn to medium and beat about 1 minute.

2. Pour batter into 2 greased and floured 8- or 9-inch round baking pans. Bake at 350°F for 30 to 35 minutes or until toothpick inserted in center comes out clean. Cool 10 minutes. Remove from pans. Cool completely on wire rack. Frost, if desired.

Chocolate Buttercream Frosting

MAKES ABOUT 4 CUPS

6 cups powdered sugar, sifted and divided

1 cup (2 sticks) butter, softened

4 to 6 squares (1 ounce each) unsweetened chocolate, melted and cooled slightly

8 to 10 tablespoons milk, divided

1 teaspoon vanilla

1. Combine 3 cups powdered sugar, butter, melted chocolate to taste, 6 tablespoons milk and vanilla in bowl of electric stand mixer. Beat at medium speed until smooth. Stop and scrape down sides

2. Add remaining 3 cups powdered sugar; beat at high speed until light and fluffy, adding more milk, 1 tablespoon at a time, as needed for good spreading consistency.

Black Bottom Cupcakes

MAKES 20 CUPCAKES

- 1 **package (8 ounces) cream cheese, softened**
- 4 **eggs**
- ⅓ **cup plus ½ cup granulated sugar, divided**
- 2 **cups all-purpose flour**
- 1 **cup packed brown sugar**
- ¾ **cup unsweetened cocoa powder**
- 1 **teaspoon baking powder**
- ½ **teaspoon baking soda**
- ½ **teaspoon salt**
- 1 **cup buttermilk**
- ½ **cup vegetable oil**
- 1½ **teaspoons vanilla**

1. Preheat oven to 350°F. Line 20 standard (2½-inch) muffin cups with paper or foil baking cups. Beat cream cheese, 1 egg and ⅓ cup granulated sugar in small bowl until smooth and creamy; set aside.

2. Combine flour, brown sugar, cocoa, remaining ½ cup granulated sugar, baking powder, baking soda and salt in bowl of electric stand mixer; mix well. Beat buttermilk, remaining 3 eggs, oil and vanilla in medium bowl until well blended. Add buttermilk mixture to mixer bowl; beat at medium speed about 2 minutes or until well blended.

3. Spoon batter into prepared muffin cups, filling about three-fourths full. Spoon heaping tablespoon cream cheese mixture over batter in each cup; gently swirl with tip of knife.

4. Bake 20 to 25 minutes or until toothpick inserted into centers comes out clean. Cool cupcakes in pans 5 minutes. Remove from pans; cool completely on wire racks.

Lazy-Daisy Cake

1. Preheat oven to 350°F. Grease 13×9-inch baking pan.

2. Place granulated sugar, eggs, 2 tablespoons butter and vanilla in bowl of electric stand mixer. Beat at medium speed 3 minutes or until fluffy. Sift flour and baking powder into medium bowl. Beat into egg mixture until well blended. Stir in milk and 2 tablespoons butter. Pour into prepared pan. Bake 30 minutes or until toothpick inserted into center comes out clean.

3. Meanwhile, combine remaining 4 tablespoons butter, coconut, brown sugar and half-and-half in medium saucepan over medium heat. Cook until sugar dissolves and butter melts, stirring constantly.

4. Spread coconut mixture over warm cake. Place under broiler, 4 inches from heat source. Broil 2 to 3 minutes or until top turns light golden brown.

MAKES 12 TO 14 SERVINGS

- 2 **cups granulated sugar**
- 4 **eggs**
- ½ **cup (1 stick) butter, softened, divided**
- 2 **teaspoon vanilla**
- 2 **cups all-purpose flour**
- 2 **teaspoons baking powder**
- 1 **cup warm milk**
- 1 **cup sweetened flaked coconut**
- ½ **cup plus 2 tablespoons packed brown sugar**
- ⅓ **cup half-and-half**

Old-Fashioned Pound Cake

MAKES 1 CAKE

- 3 cups all-purpose flour
- 2 cups sugar
- 3 teaspoons baking powder
- ½ teaspoon salt
- 2 cups (4 sticks) butter, softened
- ½ cup low-fat (1%) milk
- 1 teaspoon vanilla
- 1 teaspoon almond extract
- 6 eggs

1. Combine dry ingredients in bowl of electric stand mixer. Add butter, milk, vanilla and almond extract. Attach flat beater to mixer. Turn to low and mix about 1 minute. Stop and scrape bowl. Turn to medium and beat about 2 minutes. Stop and scrape bowl. Turn to low and add eggs, 1 at a time, mixing about 15 seconds after each addition. Turn to medium-low and beat about 30 seconds.

2. Pour batter into greased and floured 10-inch tube pan. Bake at 350°F for 1 hour 15 minutes or until toothpick inserted in center comes out clean. Cool completely in pan on wire rack. Remove cake from pan.

Banana Chocolate-Chunk Cupcakes

MAKES 20 CUPCAKES

- ½ cup (1 stick) butter, softened
- 1 cup sugar
- 2 eggs
- 3 ripe bananas, mashed
- 2 teaspoons vanilla
- 2¼ cups all-purpose flour
- 2 teaspoons baking powder
- 1 teaspoon baking soda
- ½ teaspoon ground cinnamon
- ¼ teaspoon salt
- 1 cup sour cream
- 5 (1-ounce) squares semisweet chocolate, cut into chunks
- Ganache Frosting (recipe follows)

tip

To pipe frosting rosettes on tops of cupcakes, place Ganache Frosting in pastry bag fitted with medium star tip. Gently squeeze the bag until frosting spreads around the tip. Slowly lift the bag, moving it in a circular motion as you release pressure.

1. Preheat oven to 350°F. Line 20 (2½-inch) muffin cups with paper baking cups.

2. Beat butter and sugar in bowl of electric stand mixer at medium speed until light and fluffy. Add eggs, 1 at a time, beating well after each addition. Add bananas and vanilla; beat until blended. Set aside.

3. In medium bowl, whisk together flour, baking powder, baking soda, cinnamon and salt. Gradually add flour mixture and sour cream to banana mixture, alternating additions and beating until just combined. Fold in chocolate chunks.

4. Pour batter into muffin pans, filling each cup two-thirds full. Bake 25 minutes or until toothpick inserted into centers comes out clean. Cool pans on wire racks 10 minutes. Remove cupcakes from pans; cool completely. Frost with Ganache Frosting.

Ganache Frosting

- 6 (1-ounce) squares semisweet chocolate, chopped
- 1 tablespoon vanilla
- ¾ cup whipping cream
- 2 tablespoons butter

1. Place chocolate and vanilla in bowl of food processor. In small saucepan over medium-high heat, bring cream and butter to a simmer, stirring occasionally. Remove from heat.

2. Gradually pour hot cream mixture into processor feed tube and process until smooth and thickened, about 4 minutes. Transfer to small bowl; cover with plastic wrap. Let stand at room temperature 3 hours or until spreadable.

Cookies & Cream Cupcakes

2¼ cups all-purpose flour

1 tablespoon baking powder

½ teaspoon salt

1⅔ cups sugar

1 cup milk

½ cup (1 stick) butter, softened

2 teaspoons vanilla

3 egg whites

1 cup crushed chocolate sandwich cookies (about 10 cookies), plus additional for garnish

Fluffy Frosting (see recipe on page 84)

1. Preheat oven to 350°F. Lightly grease 24 standard (2½-inch) muffin cups or line with paper baking cups.

2. Sift flour, baking powder and salt together in bowl of electric stand mixer. Stir in sugar. Add milk, butter and vanilla; mix at low speed 30 seconds. Stop and scrape bowl. Beat at medium speed 2 minutes. Add egg whites; beat 2 minutes more. Stir in 1 cup crushed cookies. Spoon batter into prepared muffin cups, filling two-thirds full.

3. Bake 20 to 25 minutes or until toothpick inserted into centers comes out clean. Cool in pans on wire racks 10 minutes. Remove cupcakes to racks; cool completely.

4. Frost cupcakes with Fluffy Frosting; garnish with additional crushed cookies.

Cookies

From brandy snaps to lemon drops, fill
your cookie jar with something special

Oatmeal S'Mores Cookies

⅔ **cup mini marshmallows**

2 **cups old-fashioned oats**

1⅓ **cups all-purpose flour**

¾ **teaspoon baking soda**

½ **teaspoon baking powder**

½ **teaspoon salt**

1 **cup packed brown sugar**

¾ **cup (1½ sticks) butter, softened**

¼ **cup granulated sugar**

1 **egg**

1 **tablespoon honey**

1 **teaspoon vanilla**

1 **cup semisweet chocolate chips**

¾ **cup coarse chocolate graham cracker crumbs**

1. Cut marshmallows in half. Spread on baking sheet; freeze 1 hour.

2. Preheat oven to 350°F. Line cookie sheets with parchment paper.

3. Combine oats, flour, baking soda, baking powder and salt in medium bowl; set aside. Beat brown sugar, butter and granulated sugar in bowl of electric stand mixer at medium speed until well blended. Beat at high speed until light and fluffy. Add egg, honey and vanilla to mixer bowl; beat at medium speed until well blended. Gradually add flour mixture; beat just until blended. Stir in chocolate chips and marshmallows.

4. Drop dough by rounded tablespoonfuls onto prepared cookie sheets; sprinkle with graham cracker crumbs. Bake 14 to 16 minutes or until puffed and golden. Cool 5 minutes on cookie sheets. Remove to wire racks to cool completely.

Variation: To make sandwich cookies, spread 1 tablespoon store-bought marshmallow crème onto flat side of 1 cookie. Spread 1 tablespoon prepared chocolate fudge frosting on flat side of second cookie. Press cookies together lightly; repeat with remaining cookies, marshmallow crème and frosting. Makes about 20 sandwiches.

Brandy Snaps with Lemon Ricotta Cream

MAKES 24 COOKIES

Cookies

- ½ **cup (1 stick) butter**
- ½ **cup sugar**
- ⅓ **cup light corn syrup**
- 1 **cup all-purpose flour**
- 1 **tablespoon brandy or cognac**

Filling

- ½ **cup (1 stick) butter, softened**
- ½ **cup ricotta cheese**
- ¼ **cup sugar**
- 2 **teaspoons grated lemon peel**
- 1 **tablespoon freshly squeezed lemon juice**

1. Preheat oven to 325°F. For cookies, place butter, sugar and corn syrup in medium saucepan over medium heat; cook and stir until butter is melted and mixture is blended. Stir in flour and brandy.

2. Drop level tablespoonfuls of batter about 3 inches apart onto ungreased cookie sheet, spacing to fit 4 cookies on sheet. Bake 1 cookie sheet at a time about 12 minutes or until golden brown.

3. When just cool enough to handle (usually within 1 minute), remove each cookie from baking sheet and quickly wrap around wooden spoon handle to form tube. (If cookies become too firm to wrap, return to oven 10 to 15 seconds to soften.)

4. For filling, place butter, ricotta, sugar, lemon peel and lemon juice in bowl of electric stand mixer. Beat at high speed until smooth.

5. Place filling in pastry bag fitted with plain or star tip, or in 1-quart food storage bag with small piece of corner cut off. Fill cookies just before serving.

Lemon Drops

MAKES ABOUT 72 COOKIES

- 2 **cups all-purpose flour**
- ⅛ **teaspoon salt**
- 1 **cup (2 sticks) butter, softened**
- 1 **cup powdered sugar, divided**
  Grated peel of 1 large lemon (about 1½ teaspoons)
- 2 **teaspoons freshly squeezed lemon juice**

1. Preheat oven to 300°F. Combine flour and salt in medium bowl.

2. Beat butter and ¾ cup powdered sugar in bowl of electric stand mixer at medium speed until fluffy. Beat in lemon peel and juice until well blended. Add flour mixture, ½ cup at a time, beating just until blended.

3. Shape dough by rounded teaspoonfuls into balls. Place 1 inch apart on ungreased cookie sheets. Bake 20 to 25 minutes or until cookies are lightly browned. Cool 5 minutes on cookie sheets; transfer to wire racks to cool completely. Sprinkle with remaining ¼ cup powdered sugar.

Soft Ginger Cookies

MAKES 30 COOKIES

  2 **cups all-purpose flour**
1½ **teaspoons ground ginger**
  1 **teaspoon baking soda**
  ¼ **teaspoon salt**
  ¼ **teaspoon ground cinnamon**
  ¼ **teaspoon ground cloves**
  ¼ **cup packed light brown sugar**
  ¼ **cup canola oil**
  ¼ **cup molasses**
  ½ **cup fat-free sour cream**
  1 **egg white**

1. Preheat oven to 350°F.

2. Combine flour, ginger, baking soda, salt, cinnamon and cloves in large bowl; set aside. Beat brown sugar, oil and molasses in bowl of electric stand mixer at medium speed 1 minute until smooth. Add sour cream and egg white; beat until well blended. Gradually add flour mixture to oil mixture, beating on low speed until well blended.

3. Drop dough by rounded tablespoonfuls 2 inches apart onto ungreased cookie sheets. Flatten dough to ⅛-inch thickness with bottom of glass lightly sprayed with nonstick cooking spray.

4. Bake 10 minutes or until tops of cookies puff up and spring back when lightly touched. Cool 2 minutes on cookie sheets. Remove to wire racks; cool completely.

Chocolate Coconut Macaroons

MAKES 20 COOKIES

1⅓ cups sweetened flaked
      coconut

⅔   cup sugar

2   egg whites

½   teaspoon vanilla

¼   teaspoon almond extract
      Pinch salt

4   ounces sliced almonds,
      coarsely crushed

20 whole almonds
      Chocolate Ganache (recipe
      follows)

1. Combine coconut, sugar, egg whites, vanilla, almond extract and salt in medium bowl; mix well. Fold in sliced almonds. Cover and refrigerate at least 1 hour or overnight.

2. Preheat oven to 350°F. Line baking sheet with parchment paper. Roll about 1 tablespoon dough into a ball. Repeat with remaining dough. Place cookies 1 inch apart on prepared sheet. Press almond on top of each cookie. Bake 15 minutes or until lightly browned. Cool cookies on pans 5 minutes. Transfer to wire rack; cool completely.

3. Meanwhile, prepare Chocolate Ganache. Let ganache cool 10 to 15 minutes.

4. Dip bottom of each cookie into ganache. Place cookies onto clean parchment or waxed paper-lined baking sheet. Refrigerate until ganache is firm.

Chocolate Ganache: Heat ½ pint whipping cream and 2 tablespoons butter in medium saucepan until just hot (do not boil). Take off heat. Add 1 (12-ounce) package semisweet chocolate chips; let stand 1 minute. Stir until smooth. Keep warm. (Ganache is semi-firm at room temperature.)

Chocolate Chip Cookies

MAKES 4½ DOZEN COOKIES

- 1 **cup granulated sugar**
- 1 **cup packed brown sugar**
- 1 **cup (2 sticks) butter, softened**
- 2 **eggs**
- 1½ **teaspoons vanilla**
- 1 **teaspoon baking soda**
- 1 **teaspoon salt**
- 3 **cups all-purpose flour**
- 12 **ounces semisweet chocolate chips**

1. Place sugars, butter, eggs and vanilla in bowl of electric stand mixer. Turn to low and mix about 30 seconds. Stop and scrape bowl. Turn to medium-low and beat about 30 seconds. Stop and scrape bowl.

2. Turn mixer to low. Gradually add baking soda, salt and flour to sugar mixture. Mix about 2 minutes. Stop and scrape bowl. Add chocolate chips. Turn to low and mix about 15 seconds more.

3. Drop rounded teaspoonfuls onto greased baking sheets, about 2 inches apart. Bake at 375°F for 10 to 12 minutes. Remove from baking sheets immediately. Cool on wire racks.

Peanut Butter Cookies

½ **cup peanut butter**
½ **cup butter, softened**
½ **cup granulated sugar**
½ **cup packed brown sugar**
1 **egg**
½ **teaspoon vanilla**
½ **teaspoon baking soda**
¼ **teaspoon salt**
1¼ **cups all-purpose flour**

tip

For a crunchier cookie with more peanut flavor, consider substituting chunky peanut butter for creamy peanut butter.

1. Place peanut butter and butter in bowl of electric stand mixer. Attach flat beater to mixer. Turn to medium and beat until mixture is smooth, about 1 minute. Stop and scrape bowl. Add sugars, egg and vanilla. Turn to medium-low and beat about 1 minute. Stop and scrape bowl.

2. Turn to low. Gradually add all remaining ingredients to sugar mixture and mix about 30 seconds.

3. Roll dough into 1-inch balls. Place balls about 2 inches apart on ungreased baking sheets. Press flat with fork in criss-cross pattern to ¼-inch thickness.

4. Bake at 375°F until golden brown, about 10 to 12 minutes. Remove from baking sheets immediately and cool on wire racks.

Deep Dark Chocolate Chip Cookies

MAKES ABOUT 30 COOKIES

2 **packages (12 ounces each) semisweet chocolate chips, divided**

½ **cup (1 stick) butter, cut into chunks**

2 **eggs**

1 **teaspoon vanilla**

¾ **cup plus 2 tablespoons sugar**

⅔ **cup all-purpose flour**

2 **tablespoons unsweetened Dutch process cocoa powder***

1 **teaspoon baking powder**

¼ **teaspoon salt**

*Dutch process cocoa powder has a mellower flavor than unsweetened cocoa powder. It is treated to neutralize its acidity, and is used in recipes that call for baking powder.

1. Lightly grease cookie sheets or line with parchment paper.

2. Combine 1 package chocolate chips and butter in large microwaveable bowl. Microwave on HIGH 30 seconds; stir. Repeat as necessary until chips are melted and mixture is smooth. Let cool slightly.

3. Beat eggs and vanilla in bowl of electric stand mixer at medium speed until blended and frothy. Add sugar; beat until thick and light. Add chocolate mixture; beat until blended. Combine flour, cocoa, baking powder and salt in medium bowl; add to butter mixture. Beat until blended. Stir in remaining 1 package chocolate chips. (Dough will be soft.)

4. Drop dough by rounded tablespoonfuls 1½ inches apart onto prepared cookie sheets. Refrigerate 30 minutes.

5. Preheat oven to 325°F. Bake 16 to 20 minutes or until cookies are firm to the touch. Cool on cookie sheets 2 minutes. Remove to wire racks; cool completely.

Almond Poppy Seed Cookies

MAKES 30 COOKIES

- ½ cup granulated sugar
- ½ cup firmly packed brown sugar
- ½ cup (1 stick) butter, softened
- 1 egg
- ½ teaspoon almond extract
- 1⅔ cups all-purpose flour
- 2 tablespoons poppy seeds
- 1 teaspoon baking powder
- ¼ teaspoon salt
- ½ cup unblanched chopped almonds

1. Place granulated sugar, brown sugar and butter in bowl of electric stand mixer. Turn to medium-low and beat 1 minute. Continuing on medium-low, add egg and almond extract and beat 1 minute more. In separate bowl, combine flour, poppy seeds, baking powder and salt. Turn mixer to low and add flour mixture, mixing just until combined.

2. Shape dough into 1-inch balls, roll in chopped almonds and place on greased baking sheets. Bake at 375°F for 10 to 12 minutes or until lightly browned. Cool on wire racks.

Brown Edge Wafers

MAKES 24 COOKIES

- ½ **cup (1 stick) butter, softened**
- ½ **cup sugar**
- 1 **egg**
- 1 **teaspoon vanilla**
- ½ **teaspoon grated orange peel**
- 1 **cup all-purpose flour**

tip

When the cookies have cooled, drizzle them with melted chocolate for a special finishing touch.

1. Place butter and sugar in bowl of electric stand mixer. Turn to medium and beat 15 seconds. Stop and scrape bowl.

2. Add egg, vanilla and orange peel. Turn to medium and beat 30 seconds. Stop and scrape bowl. Turn to low and add flour, mixing 15 seconds or just until blended.

3. Drop by teaspoonfuls onto greased baking sheets. Bake at 375°F for 8 to 10 minutes. Cool on wire racks.

Coconut Almond Biscotti

MAKES 24 BISCOTTI

2½ cups all-purpose flour

1⅓ cups unsweetened flaked coconut

¾ cup sliced almonds

⅔ cup sugar

2 teaspoons baking powder

½ teaspoon salt

1 extra-large egg at room temperature

1 extra-large egg white at room temperature

½ cup (1 stick) butter, melted

1 teaspoon vanilla

1. Center rack in oven and preheat to 350°F. Line baking sheet with parchment paper or nonstick liner.

2. Combine flour, coconut, almonds, sugar, baking powder and salt in bowl of electric stand mixer. Mix at low speed 2 minutes or just until combined.

3. Lightly beat together egg, egg white, butter and vanilla in separate mixing bowl. Turn mixer to low. Add egg mixture to dry ingredients. Blend together.

4. Divide dough into 2 equal pieces. Dust hands lightly with flour and shape each piece of dough into 1 (8×3×¾-inch) loaf. Place loaves on baking sheet, leaving several inches between them.

5. Bake loaves 26 to 28 minutes or until golden and set. Remove baking pan from oven and cool on rack 10 minutes. Using a serrated bread knife, slice each loaf on the diagonal into ½-inch-thick slices. Place slices on their sides on baking sheets. Bake 20 minutes or until firm and golden. Remove from oven and cool on rack.

Pecan Shortbread Cookies

1. Place butter, vanilla and brown sugar in bowl of electric stand mixer. Attach flat beater to mixer. Turn to medium and beat 1 minute. Stop and scrape bowl.

2. Turn to low and add flour; beat 30 seconds. Stop and scrape bowl. Turn to low and quickly add pecans, mixing just until blended.

3. Shape dough into log 1½ inches in diameter. Wrap in waxed paper and chill 20 minutes. Slice dough into ½-inch-thick cookies. Place cookies on greased baking sheets. Bake at 325°F for 18 to 20 minutes. Cool on wire racks.

MAKES 2 DOZEN COOKIES

- 1 **cup (2 sticks) butter**
- 1 **teaspoon vanilla**
- ¾ **cup packed brown sugar**
- 2½ **cups all-purpose flour**
- ½ **cup chopped pecans**

tip

Soft cookies should be stored between layers of waxed paper in an airtight container. A piece of apple or bread, changed frequently, will help keep cookies soft. Store crisp cookies in an airtight container with a loose-fitting lid. If they soften, place in oven at 300°F for 3 to 5 minutes before serving.

New England Raisin Spice Cookies

MAKES 60 COOKIES

1 cup packed brown sugar

½ cup shortening

¼ cup (½ stick) butter

1 egg

⅓ cup molasses

2¼ cups all-purpose flour

2 teaspoons baking soda

1 teaspoon salt

¾ teaspoon ground cinnamon

¼ teaspoon ground ginger

¼ teaspoon ground cloves

⅛ teaspoon ground allspice

1½ cups raisins

Granulated sugar

1. Beat brown sugar, shortening and butter in bowl of electric stand mixer at medium speed until creamy. Add egg and molasses; beat until fluffy.

2. Combine all remaining ingredients except granulated sugar in separate bowl. Gradually stir into shortening mixture until just blended. Cover; refrigerate at least 2 hours.

3. Preheat oven to 350°F.

4. Scoop heaping tablespoonfuls of dough; roll into smooth balls. Roll in granulated sugar. Place on ungreased cookie sheets 1½ to 2 inches apart. Bake 8 to 10 minutes or until golden brown. Cool 1 minute on cookie sheets. Remove to wire racks; cool completely. Store in airtight container.

Lightly Spiced Benne Sesame Cookies

1. Preheat oven to 375°F. Coat nonstick cookie sheets with nonstick cooking spray; set aside.

2. Blend flour, baking powder, cinnamon, nutmeg, salt and sesame seeds in small bowl. Cream sugar and butter in bowl of electric stand mixer until light and fluffy. Add egg yolks, vinegar and vanilla; beat well. Add flour mixture; beat well.

3. Drop dough by rounded teaspoonfuls 2 inches apart on prepared cookie sheets. Gently flatten cookies slightly with a fork.

4. Bake 5 to 6 minutes or until edges are just golden. Remove from heat. Cool 1 minute on cookie sheet; transfer cookies to wire rack to cool completely.

MAKES 36 COOKIES

- ½ **cup all-purpose flour**
- ½ **teaspoon baking powder**
- ½ **to 1 teaspoon ground cinnamon**
- ½ **teaspoon ground nutmeg**
- ¼ **teaspoon salt**
- 1 **cup sesame seeds, toasted**
- ½ **cup packed light brown sugar**
- 2 **tablespoons butter, softened**
- 2 **egg yolks**
- 1 **teaspoon cider vinegar**
- ½ **teaspoon vanilla**

tip

Benne is the African synonym for sesame. Benne seeds are considered good luck, so Benne cookies are a popular treat for holidays and celebrations.

PB & J Thumbprint Cookies

2 cups old-fashioned oats

1⅓ cups plus 1 tablespoon all-purpose flour

¾ teaspoon baking soda

½ teaspoon baking powder

½ teaspoon salt

1 cup packed brown sugar

¾ cup (1½ sticks) butter, softened

¼ cup granulated sugar

¼ cup chunky peanut butter

1 egg

1 tablespoon honey

1 teaspoon vanilla

½ cup chopped peanuts, unsalted or honey-roasted

½ cup grape jelly or flavor of choice

1. Preheat oven to 350°F. Line cookie sheets with parchment paper.

2. Combine oats, flour, baking soda, baking powder and salt in medium bowl. Beat brown sugar, butter and granulated sugar in bowl of electric stand mixer at medium speed until well blended. Beat at high speed until light and fluffy. Add peanut butter, egg, honey and vanilla; beat at medium speed until well blended. Gradually add flour mixture; beat just until blended. Stir in peanuts.

3. Drop dough by rounded tablespoonfuls onto prepared cookie sheets. Bake 10 minutes. Remove cookies from oven. Press center of each cookie with back of teaspoon to make a slight indentation; fill with about ½ teaspoon jelly. Return to oven; bake 4 to 6 minutes or until puffed and golden. Cool 5 minutes on cookie sheets; remove to wire racks to cool completely.

Carrot Cake Cookies

MAKES 36 COOKIES

1½ cups all-purpose flour

1 teaspoon ground cinnamon

½ teaspoon baking soda

½ teaspoon salt

¾ cup packed brown sugar

½ cup (1 stick) butter, softened

1 egg

½ teaspoon vanilla

1 cup grated carrots (about 2 medium carrots)

½ cup chopped walnuts

½ cup raisins or chopped dried pineapple (optional)

1. Preheat oven to 350°F. Grease cookie sheets or line with parchment paper.

2. Combine flour, cinnamon, baking soda and salt in medium bowl; set aside. Beat brown sugar and butter in bowl of electric stand mixer until creamy. Add egg and vanilla; beat until well blended. Stir in flour mixture; mix well. Stir in carrots, walnuts and raisins, if desired. Drop dough by rounded tablespoonfuls 2 inches apart onto prepared cookie sheets.

3. Bake 12 to 14 minutes or until set and edges are lightly browned. Cool on cookie sheets 1 minute. Remove to wire racks to cool completely.

Cocoa and Peanut Butter Yummies

MAKES 48 COOKIES

1⅓ cups all-purpose flour

½ cup unsweetened cocoa
   powder

¾ teaspoon baking soda

¼ teaspoon salt

¾ cup (1½ sticks) butter,
   softened

½ cup granulated sugar

½ cup packed brown sugar

1 egg

2 tablespoons water

½ teaspoon vanilla

1 package (12 ounces) peanut
   butter chips

1. Preheat oven to 375°F. Combine flour, cocoa, baking soda and salt in medium bowl; set aside.

2. Beat butter, granulated sugar and brown sugar in bowl of electric stand mixer at medium speed until smooth and creamy. Add egg, water and vanilla; beat 2 minutes. Add flour mixture; beat until well blended. Add peanut butter chips; mix at low speed 30 seconds. Drop dough by rounded tablespoonfuls 3 inches apart onto ungreased cookie sheets.

3. Bake 8 to 10 minutes or until firm in center. Do not overbake. Remove to wire racks to cool completely.

Desserts

Dare to explore the decadent world
of soufflés, brûlées, and beyond

Cherry-Almond Clafouti

MAKES 4 SERVINGS

- ½ **cup slivered almonds, toasted***
- ½ **cup powdered sugar**
- ⅔ **cup all-purpose flour**
- ⅔ **cup granulated sugar**
- ¼ **teaspoon salt**
- ½ **cup (1 stick) butter, cut into pieces**
- ⅔ **cup milk**
- 2 **eggs**
- ½ **teaspoon vanilla**
- 1 **cup fresh cherries, pitted and quartered**

To toast almonds, spread in single layer on baking sheet. Bake in preheated 350°F oven 8 to 10 minutes or until golden brown, stirring frequently.

1. Preheat oven to 350°F. Spray 4 (6-ounce) ramekins with nonstick cooking spray; place on baking sheet.

2. Process almonds in food processor until coarsely ground. Add powdered sugar; pulse until well blended. Add flour, granulated sugar and salt. Pulse until well blended. Gradually add butter, pulsing just until blended.

3. Combine milk, eggs and vanilla in small bowl. With food processor running, gradually add milk mixture to almond mixture. Process until blended. Remove blade from food processor; stir in cherries.

4. Divide batter among prepared ramekins. Bake about 50 minutes or until tops and sides are puffy and golden. Let cool 5 to 10 minutes.

Note: Clafouti is a traditional French dessert made by layering a sweet batter over fresh fruit. The result is a rich dessert with a cake-like topping and pudding-like center.

Individual English Trifles

MAKES 6 TRIFLES

Hot-Milk Sponge Sheet Cake

- **Butter**
- **Powdered sugar**
- 1 **cup all-purpose flour**
- 1 **teaspoon baking powder**
- ⅓ **cup milk**
- 2 **tablespoons butter**
- ½ **teaspoon vanilla**
- 6 **large eggs**
- 1 **cup granulated sugar**

Mascarpone Custard

- 3 **large egg yolks**
- ¼ **cup granulated sugar**
- 2 **tablespoons heavy cream**
- 2 **tablespoons cream sherry**
- 8 **ounces mascarpone**

Trifle Filling

- 1 **cup raspberries**
- 1 **cup sliced strawberries**
- 1 **tablespoon granulated sugar**
- ½ **cup heavy whipping cream**
- 1 **tablespoon powdered sugar**
- 1 **teaspoon vanilla**
- 6 **short, straight-sided glasses**
- ⅓ **cup cream sherry, for brushing cake**
- ¾ **cup raspberry jam**

1. For Hot-Milk Sponge Sheet Cake, preheat oven to 350°F. Generously grease 11×17-inch jellyroll pan with butter; dust with powdered sugar. Sift flour and baking powder into bowl. Return mixture to sifter. Heat milk, butter and vanilla in small saucepan over low heat. Combine eggs and granulated sugar in bowl of electric stand mixer. Beat at high speed until mixture becomes pale yellow and triples in volume.

2. Gently fold warm milk mixture into egg mixture. Sift flour and baking powder into egg and milk mixture in 4 parts, stirring at low speed after each addition until batter is smooth. Pour batter evenly into baking pan. Bake 15 to 17 minutes or until cake is lightly browned and center springs back when touched. Cool 5 minutes.

3. Dust large piece of parchment paper with powdered sugar. Run knife around cake edges to loosen, and then overturn onto parchment. Cool.

4. For Mascarpone Custard, beat egg yolks, granulated sugar, cream and sherry in medium heatproof bowl 2 minutes. Fill saucepan with 1 inch water and simmer over medium-low heat. Set bowl tightly over saucepan so that bottom of bowl rests at least 1 inch from water. Heat egg mixture, stirring and scraping down sides of bowl often, until it reaches 160°F, about 5 to 7 minutes. Remove from heat. Add mascarpone to egg mixture and beat until smooth; set aside.

5. To assemble trifles, combine berries and granulated sugar; set aside. Whip cream, powdered sugar and vanilla in bowl of electric stand mixer at high speed until stiff peaks form; set aside.

6. Using rim of 1 glass, cut out 18 sponge cake circles. Brush each generously with cream sherry.

7. Place 1 cake piece in bottom of each glass. Spread cake with 1 to 2 teaspoons raspberry jam. Spread 2 tablespoons Mascarpone Custard over jam. Drop 2 tablespoons fruit over custard. Repeat layering cake, jam, custard and fruit.

8. Top each glass with third cake circle and 2 to 3 tablespoons whipped cream. Garnish with berries. Cover and refrigerate at least 2 hours or overnight before serving.

Raspberry-Chocolate Empanadas

MAKES 8 TO 10 EMPANADAS

- 2 **cups all-purpose flour**
- 1 **teaspoon salt**
- 1 **tablespoon packed brown sugar**
- ½ **cup (1 stick) butter**
- 5 **tablespoons buttermilk**
- 2 **cups raspberries**
- 1 **teaspoon freshly squeezed lemon juice**
- ½ **cup granulated sugar**
- 3 **tablespoons cornstarch, plus extra for dusting**
- 2 **ounces semisweet chocolate, finely chopped**
- 1 **egg beaten with 1 tablespoon milk**

1. For empanada dough, combine flour, salt and brown sugar in medium bowl. Using pastry blender or 2 knives, cut in butter until mixture resembles coarse meal.

2. Add buttermilk 1 tablespoon at a time, stirring to moisten ingredients, until dough forms. Gather dough into ball. Wrap in plastic and refrigerate 30 minutes.

3. For filling, gently mix raspberries, lemon juice, granulated sugar, cornstarch and chocolate until berries are uniformly coated.

4. Remove chilled dough and roll into circle ¼ inch thick. Cut into approximate 5-inch circles, rerolling dough once to yield 8 to 10 empanadas.

5. Brush dough circles on 1 side with egg/milk mixture. Dust with cornstarch. Drop 1 tablespoon filling onto center of each dough circle. Fold 1 side over to form half-circle shape. Pinch edges closed and crimp with fork to seal. Brush edges and tops with egg/milk mixture. Cut decorative slits into top of empanadas, if desired.

6. Preheat oven to 425°F. Line baking sheet with parchment paper. Arrange empanadas 2 inches apart; chill 15 minutes. Bake 15 to 20 minutes or until golden brown. Cool on rack 10 minutes before serving.

Note: Empanada is a traditional Latin-American dish made from pastry and a variety of sweet or savory fillings.

Double Chocolate Bombe

5   eggs, separated

1½ cups whipping cream, divided

1   envelope unflavored gelatin

1   package (12 ounces) semisweet chocolate chips

¼   teaspoon salt

⅓   cup sugar

Chocolate Cake (recipe follows)

1   white chocolate baking bar (2 ounces)

White Chocolate Cut-Outs (recipe follows, optional)

1. Line 2-quart bowl with plastic wrap; lightly oil.

2. For mousse, place egg yolks and ½ cup whipping cream in small bowl; beat slightly with fork. Sprinkle gelatin over egg yolk mixture. Let stand without stirring 5 minutes to soften.

3. Melt chocolate chips in top of double boiler over hot, not boiling, water. Stir about ½ cup melted chocolate into egg yolk mixture. Stir egg yolk mixture back into remaining chocolate in top of double boiler. Continue to heat until gelatin is completely dissolved.

4. Beat egg whites and salt in bowl of electric stand mixer at high speed until foamy. Gradually beat in sugar until stiff peaks form. (After beaters are lifted from egg white mixture, stiff peaks should remain on top, and when bowl is tilted, mixture will not slide around.) Fold chocolate mixture into egg white mixture with rubber spatula.

5. Beat 1 cup whipping cream until soft peaks form; fold into chocolate mixture. Pour into prepared bowl. Cover and refrigerate 4 hours.

6. For bombe, place cake on serving plate. Unmold mousse onto cake. Remove plastic wrap. Trim edge of cake around mousse, if necessary.

7. Place white chocolate baking bar in small resealable freezer bag. Microwave on MEDIUM 2 minutes. Turn bag over; microwave on MEDIUM 2 to 3 minutes or until chocolate is melted. Knead bag until chocolate is smooth. Cut off very tiny corner of bag; drizzle chocolate over mousse. Refrigerate until white chocolate is set, about 30 minutes. Garnish, if desired.

Note: Bombe is a traditional dome-shaped frozen or molded French dessert.

Chocolate Cake

1. Preheat oven to 375°F. Grease and flour bottom and sides of 9-inch round baking pan. Gently tap side of pan to evenly coat bottom and sides.

2. Combine sugar and shortening in bowl of electric stand mixer. Beat at medium speed until light and fluffy, scraping down sides of bowl once. Add eggs, water and vanilla; beat well.

3. Combine flour, cocoa, baking soda, baking powder and salt in small bowl. Add to shortening mixture; beat at medium speed until smooth. Pour batter into prepared pan.

4. Bake 20 to 25 minutes or until cake tester or toothpick inserted into center comes out clean. Cool 10 minutes in pan.

5. Loosen edges and remove to wire rack; cool completely.

MAKES 1 CAKE

1 **cup sugar**

⅓ **cup shortening**

2 **eggs**

⅓ **cup water**

½ **teaspoon vanilla**

1 **cup all-purpose flour**

⅓ **cup unsweetened cocoa powder**

1 **teaspoon baking soda**

¼ **teaspoon baking powder**

¼ **teaspoon salt**

White Chocolate Cut-Outs

2 **white chocolate baking bars (2 ounces each), coarsely chopped**

1. Melt chocolate in small bowl set in bowl of very hot water, stirring occasionally, about 10 minutes.

2. Pour chocolate onto waxed paper-lined cookie sheet. Refrigerate until firm, about 15 minutes.

3. Cut out large triangle shapes with sharp knife.

4. Immediately lift shapes carefully from waxed paper with spatula or knife. Refrigerate until ready to use.

Individual Chocolate Soufflés

MAKES 2 SERVINGS

1   teaspoon unsalted butter, divided

5   tablespoons granulated sugar, divided

4   ounces semisweet chocolate, chopped

2   ounces cream cheese, softened

2   tablespoons milk

2   large eggs, separated, at room temperature

    Pinch salt

    Powdered sugar

tip

Place soufflés in the oven just before serving your meal; soufflés will be ready when it's time for dessert and coffee.

1. Use ½ teaspoon butter to grease 2 (10-ounce) custard cups; coat with 1 tablespoon granulated sugar.

2. Make collars for custard cups: fold 2 (16-inch-long) pieces of foil in half lengthwise, and fold in half again. Use remaining ½ teaspoon butter to grease one side of each collar. Sprinkle each buttered side with 1½ teaspoons granulated sugar. Wrap each collar around custard cup, buttered side in; allow collars to extend above the rim 1 inch. If necessary, secure with masking tape.

3. Preheat oven to 350°F. Place baking pan in oven. Microwave chocolate, cream cheese and milk in microwaveable container on HIGH 1 minute. Stir until smooth. If mixture is not completely melted, return to microwave oven and heat in 30-second intervals, stirring each time. Allow mixture to cool, then stir in yolks and blend well.

4. Beat egg whites in bowl of electric stand mixer at high speed until frothy. Add salt, then gradually add remaining 3 tablespoons granulated sugar, beating constantly, until stiff peaks form.

5. Gently fold chocolate mixture into whites in 3 additions. Divide between custard cups.

6. Place custard cups on preheated baking pan. Bake 35 to 40 minutes or until puffed and toothpick inserted in middle comes out clean. Dust with powdered sugar. Remove collars and serve immediately (soufflés deflate as they cool).

Note: Soufflés have an undeserved reputation of being hard to make. The cream cheese in this recipe helps to stabilize the soufflé and gives it a subtle flavor note.

Panettone Bread Pudding with Caramel Sauce

MAKES 12 SERVINGS

1 tablespoon butter, softened

½ (2 pound) loaf panettone bread, cut into ¾-inch pieces (see recipe on page 50)

6 eggs

½ cup sugar

3 cups half-and-half

1 teaspoon vanilla

½ teaspoon ground cinnamon

¼ teaspoon salt

Caramel ice cream topping

1. Preheat oven to 350°F. Grease 11×7-inch baking dish with butter.

2. Arrange bread in dish. Combine eggs and sugar in large bowl; whisk in half-and-half, vanilla, cinnamon and salt. Pour mixture over bread; press down to moisten bread tops. Let stand 15 minutes.

3. Bake 40 to 45 minutes or until puffed and golden brown. Serve warm or at room temperature. Drizzle with caramel ice cream topping.

Serving Suggestion: Dust lightly with powdered sugar and serve caramel topping on the side.

Pineapple-Rum Napoleons

MAKES 4 NAPOLEONS

- 1 **package puff pastry, thawed and cut into 12 (3-inch) rounds**
- 3 **egg yolks**
- ½ **cup mango nectar***
- 1 **tablespoon granulated sugar**
- 2 **teaspoons cornstarch**
- ⅔ **cup milk**
- 6 **tablespoons butter**
- 1 **large pineapple, peeled and cut into 8 slices, about ½ inch thick**
- ⅔ **cup packed brown sugar**
- ⅔ **cup water**
- ½ **cup dark rum**
- ½ **teaspoon vanilla**

   Powdered sugar (optional)

Canned mango nectar is sold in the international or ethnic food sections at most supermarkets.

1. Preheat oven to 400°F. Place rounds on parchment-lined baking sheet and bake until puffed and golden brown, about 13 minutes.

2. For pastry cream, whisk together yolks, nectar, granulated sugar and cornstarch in small bowl. Bring milk to a simmer in small saucepan over medium-low heat. Slowly whisk hot milk into egg mixture, stirring constantly. Return mixture to medium-low heat. Whisk constantly until thick, about 6 minutes. Strain through fine-meshed strainer, using a rubber spatula to push cream down as it strains. Cover with plastic wrap and chill until ready to use.

3. For sauce, heat 2 large skillets over medium-high heat. Melt 3 tablespoons butter in each skillet. Add pineapple slices in single layer and brown lightly on both sides. Gently stir in brown sugar and water (dividing equally between 2 pans), reduce heat to medium-low and simmer 10 minutes or until pineapple is soft.

4. Remove pineapple from pans and combine all sauce into 1 pan. Add rum. Cook, stirring frequently, until sauce reduces, about 5 minutes. Stir in vanilla.

5. Remove cores of pineapple slices using small cookie cutter. Spoon 3 tablespoons sauce onto plate. Place 1 puff pastry round on sauce and top with 1 tablespoon pastry cream. Top cream with pineapple slice, followed by another tablespoon of cream and puff pastry round. Repeat layers. Sprinkle with powdered sugar.

Pumpkin Flans

1 **can (15 ounces) solid-pack pumpkin**

1 **can (12 ounces) evaporated milk**

1⅔ **cups granulated sugar, divided**

3 **eggs**

2 **teaspoons vanilla, divided**

1 **teaspoon ground cinnamon**

½ **teaspoon ground ginger**

½ **teaspoon ground nutmeg**

½ **teaspoon ground cloves**

¼ **cup whipping cream**

1 **tablespoon powdered sugar**

1. Preheat oven to 300°F. Beat pumpkin, evaporated milk, ⅓ cup granulated sugar, eggs, 1 teaspoon vanilla, cinnamon, ginger, nutmeg and cloves in bowl of electric stand mixer at medium speed until blended.

2. Place remaining 1⅓ cups granulated sugar in large saucepan over medium-high heat; cook until melted and golden brown. (Mixture will be very hot.) Carefully pour sugar into 8 (4-ounce) ramekins. Fill each ramekin with pumpkin mixture; place in 15×11-inch baking dish. Pour hot water into dish halfway up sides of ramekins.

3. Bake 45 to 55 minutes or until knife inserted into centers comes out clean. Let cool. Run knife around edges of ramekins to loosen flans. Invert flans onto serving plates.

4. Beat whipping cream, powdered sugar and remaining 1 teaspoon vanilla in bowl of electric stand mixer at high speed until soft peaks form; spoon onto flans.

Variation: Flan can also be baked in 9-inch pie pan for 60 minutes.

Chocolate Crème Brûlée

- 2 **cups whipping cream**
- 3 **squares semisweet or bittersweet baking chocolate, finely chopped**
- 3 **egg yolks**
- ¼ **cup granulated sugar**
- 2 **teaspoons vanilla**
- 3 **tablespoons packed brown sugar**

1. Preheat oven to 325°F. Heat cream in medium saucepan over medium heat until it just begins to simmer (do not boil). Remove pan from heat; stir in chocolate until melted and smooth. Set aside to cool slightly.

2. Beat egg yolks and granulated sugar in bowl of electric stand mixer at medium-high speed about 5 minutes or until mixture thickens and becomes pale in color. Whisk in chocolate mixture and vanilla until well blended.

3. Divide mixture among 4 (6-ounce) custard cups or individual baking dishes. Place cups in baking pan; place pan in oven. Pour boiling water into baking pan to reach halfway up sides of custard cups. Cover pan loosely with foil.

4. Bake 30 minutes or until edges are just set. Remove cups from baking pan to wire rack to cool completely. Wrap with plastic wrap and refrigerate 4 hours or up to 3 days.

5. When ready to serve, preheat broiler. Spread 2 teaspoons brown sugar evenly over each cup. Broil 3 to 4 minutes, watching carefully, until sugar bubbles and browns. Serve immediately.

Hidden Pumpkin Pies

MAKES 6 SERVINGS

1½ cups solid-pack pumpkin

1 cup evaporated fat-free (skim) milk

½ cup cholesterol-free egg substitute

¼ cup no-calorie sugar substitute

1¼ teaspoons vanilla, divided

1 teaspoon pumpkin pie spice*

3 egg whites

¼ teaspoon cream of tartar

⅓ cup honey

Substitute ½ teaspoon ground cinnamon, ¼ teaspoon ground ginger, and ⅛ teaspoon each ground allspice and ground nutmeg for 1 teaspoon pumpkin pie spice, if desired.

1. Preheat oven to 350°F.

2. Combine pumpkin, evaporated milk, egg substitute, sugar substitute, 1 teaspoon vanilla and pumpkin pie spice in large bowl. Pour into 6 (6-ounce) custard cups or soufflé dishes. Place in shallow baking dish or pan. Pour boiling water around custard cups to depth of 1 inch. Bake 25 minutes or until set.

3. Meanwhile, beat egg whites, cream of tartar and remaining ¼ teaspoon vanilla in bowl of electric stand mixer at high speed until soft peaks form. Gradually add honey, beating until stiff peaks form.

4. Spread egg white mixture over hot pumpkin pies. Return to oven. Bake 8 to 12 minutes or until tops of pies are golden brown. Let stand 10 minutes. Serve warm.

Shortcake with Blueberry Sauce

Shortcake

- 1 **cup all-purpose flour**
- ¼ **teaspoon salt**
- 2 **teaspoons baking powder**
- 4 **teaspoons sugar**
- ¼ **cup (½ stick) unsalted butter, thinly sliced**
- 6 **to 8 tablespoons milk**

Blueberry Sauce

- 2 **cups fresh blueberries***
- 3 **tablespoons sugar**
  Grated peel of 1 small lemon
- 1 **tablespoon lemon juice**
- 2 **tablespoons water**

Blueberry-Cream Topping

- ⅔ **cup whipping cream**
- 1 **tablespoon sugar**
- ¾ **cup fresh blueberries, plus additional for garnish**

Or use 2 cups frozen thawed blueberries and reduce water to 1 tablespoon.

1. Preheat oven to 425°F.

2. For Shortcake, stir flour, salt, baking powder and sugar together in medium bowl. Add butter; cut in with pastry blender or 2 knives until mixture resembles coarse crumbs. Add milk by the tablespoon, stirring gently until dough comes together (dough will be slightly sticky). Knead gently 4 to 6 times.

3. Divide dough into 4 pieces. Shape into 2½-inch rounds, about ¾ inch high. Place on ungreased baking sheet. Bake 15 minutes or until golden brown. Remove biscuits from oven; place on wire rack to cool.

4. For Blueberry Sauce, combine blueberries, sugar, lemon peel, lemon juice and water in small saucepan. Bring to a boil over high heat; reduce heat. Cover and simmer 10 minutes, stirring occasionally, or until berries are tender and sauce has thickened.

5. For Blueberry-Cream Topping, whip cream and sugar in bowl of electric stand mixer at medium-high speed until stiff. Fold in blueberries.

6. To assemble, split each biscuit in half. Spoon about ¼ cup Blueberry Sauce on bottom half of each biscuit. Replace biscuit tops. Spoon about ½ cup Blueberry-Cream Topping onto each shortcake. Garnish with additional blueberries.

Creamy Apple Phyllo Purses

MAKES 10 PURSES

2 medium Granny Smith apples, finely diced

¼ cup packed brown sugar

1 tablespoon butter

½ teaspoon ground cinnamon

⅛ teaspoon ground cloves

6 ounces cream cheese, softened

15 sheets frozen phyllo dough, thawed

⅔ cup butter, melted

⅔ cup raspberry preserves or fruit spread, melted

Powdered sugar

1. Combine apples, brown sugar, butter, cinnamon and cloves in medium saucepan; cook and stir over medium-high heat 3 minutes. Remove from heat; stir in cream cheese until completely blended. Spread mixture in shallow pan; place in freezer 15 minutes to chill.

2. Preheat oven to 350°F. Stack 3 sheets phyllo on clean work surface or cutting board, brushing each with melted butter before adding next sheet. Cut phyllo stack in half crosswise to form 2 rectangles. Repeat with remaining phyllo dough to create total of 10 rectangles.

3. Place scant ¼ cup chilled apple filling in center of each rectangle. Lightly brush phyllo dough around filling with water. Gather corners of rectangle and pinch together just above filling. Arrange purses on ungreased baking sheet at least 1 inch apart; brush with melted butter.

4. Bake 18 to 20 minutes or until golden brown. (Some filling may leak out.) Spoon melted preserves on individual dessert plates. Place purses over preserves; sprinkle with powdered sugar.

Apricot Dessert Soufflé

MAKES 6 SERVINGS

- 3 **tablespoons butter**
- 2 **tablespoons all-purpose flour**
- 1 **cup apricot no-sugar-added pourable fruit***
- ⅓ **cup finely chopped dried apricots**
- 3 **egg yolks, beaten**
- 4 **egg whites**
- ¼ **teaspoon cream of tartar**
- ⅛ **teaspoon salt**
- **Whipped cream**

Or substitute ¾ cup apricot fruit spread mixed with ¼ cup warm water.

1. Preheat oven to 325°F. Melt butter in medium saucepan. Add flour; cook and stir until bubbly. Add pourable fruit and apricots; cook and stir 3 minutes or until thickened. Remove from heat; whisk in egg yolks. Cool to room temperature, stirring occasionally.

2. Beat egg whites, cream of tartar and salt in bowl of electric stand mixer at high speed until stiff peaks form. Gently fold egg white mixture into apricot mixture. Spoon into 1½-quart soufflé dish. Bake 30 minutes or until puffed and golden brown. Top with whipped cream. Serve immediately.

Rustic Cranberry-Pear Galette

MAKES 8 SERVINGS

- ¼ cup sugar, divided
- 1 tablespoon plus 1 teaspoon cornstarch
- 2 teaspoons ground cinnamon or apple pie spice
- 4 cups thinly sliced, peeled Bartlett pears
- ¼ cup dried cranberries
- 1 teaspoon vanilla
- ¼ teaspoon almond extract (optional)
- 1 Perfect Pie Pastry shell, unbaked (see recipe on page 194)
- 1 egg white
- 1 tablespoon water

1. Preheat oven to 450°F. Coat pizza pan or baking sheet with nonstick cooking spray.

2. Reserve 1 teaspoon sugar. Combine remaining sugar, cornstarch and cinnamon in medium bowl; mix well. Add pears, cranberries, vanilla and almond extract, if desired; toss to coat.

3. Place pie shell on prepared pan. Spoon pear mixture into center of crust to within 2 inches of edge. Fold edge of crust 2 inches over pear mixture; crimp slightly.

4. Whisk egg white and water in small bowl until well blended. Brush outer edge of pie crust with egg white mixture; sprinkle with reserved 1 teaspoon sugar.

5. Bake 25 minutes or until pears are tender and crust is golden brown. If edge browns too quickly, cover with foil after 15 minutes of baking. Cool on wire rack 30 minutes.

Apple Fritters with Two Sauces

Apple Fritters

Peanut oil or vegetable oil for deep frying

1 cup whole milk

¼ cup unsalted butter, melted

Freshly grated peel and juice of 1 large orange

1 egg

1 teaspoon vanilla

1 large tart apple, peeled, cored and chopped

3 cups sifted all-purpose flour

½ cup granulated sugar

1 tablespoon baking powder

½ teaspoon salt

Powdered sugar

Strawberry Sauce

1 package (12 ounces) frozen unsweetened strawberries, thawed

Butterscotch Sauce

6 tablespoons unsalted butter

¼ cup granulated sugar

¼ cup packed dark brown sugar

⅔ cup whipping cream

1½ tablespoons lemon juice

1 teaspoon vanilla

½ teaspoon salt

1. For Apple Fritters, heat 2 to 2½ inches oil in heavy saucepan over medium-high heat until deep-fry thermometer registers 350°F; adjust heat to maintain temperature.

2. Combine milk, butter, orange peel, juice, egg and vanilla in bowl of electric stand mixer; beat until well blended. Stir in apple. Combine flour, sugar, baking powder and salt in medium bowl; gradually stir into milk mixture until blended. (Batter will be thick.)

3. Drop batter by ¼ cupfuls into hot oil. Fry 3 to 4 fritters at a time 8 to 10 minutes, turning often, until evenly browned and crisp. Drain on paper towels.

4. For Strawberry Sauce, process strawberries in blender until smooth.

5. For Butterscotch Sauce, melt butter in small saucepan over medium-high heat. Add sugars; stir until melted. Stir in cream; simmer 2 minutes. Remove from heat; stir in lemon juice, vanilla and salt.

6. Place fritters on serving platter; dust with powdered sugar. Serve with Strawberry and Butterscotch Sauces for dipping.

Profiteroles with Apricot Pastry Cream

MAKES 18 PROFITEROLES

- 1 **cup all-purpose flour**
- 1/8 **teaspoon salt**
- 1 **cup water**
- 1/3 **cup butter**
- 1 **teaspoon vanilla**
- 4 **eggs, at room temperature**
- **Apricot Pastry Cream (recipe follows)**
- **Raspberry Coulis (recipe follows, optional)**
- **Fresh raspberry leaves (optional)**

1. Preheat oven to 400°F. Combine flour and salt in medium bowl; set aside. Bring water and butter to a boil in heavy medium saucepan over medium-high heat. Add flour mixture all at once; beat vigorously until dough leaves sides of pan and forms smooth ball. Remove from heat; let stand 2 minutes. Beat in vanilla. Beat in eggs, 1 at a time. Drop heaping tablespoonfuls of dough, 2 inches apart, onto lightly greased cookie sheets. Bake 10 minutes. Reduce oven temperature to 350°F. Continue baking 25 minutes or until golden brown. (Do not open oven door during baking.) Cool completely on wire racks.

2. Just before serving, prepare Apricot Pastry Cream. Cut cream puffs in half horizontally with serrated knife. Remove soft dough from center of puffs; discard. Fill puffs with pastry cream; replace tops. Serve with Raspberry Coulis and garnish with fresh raspberry leaves, if desired.

Apricot Pastry Cream

Beat 1/2 cup whipping cream at high speed in bowl of electric stand mixer until soft peaks form. Combine 6 ounces whipped cream cheese and 1/2 cup no-sugar-added apricot fruit spread in medium bowl; mix until well blended. Fold into whipped cream.

Raspberry Coulis

Place 2 cups fresh raspberries in blender container; cover and blend until smooth. Strain; discard seeds. Combine purée, 1/2 cup no-sugar-added seedless raspberry fruit spread and 1 1/2 tablespoons orange liqueur, if desired; mix well.

Dreamy Orange Cream Puffs

1. Prepare Cream Puffs.

2. Combine granulated sugar, cornstarch and orange juice in medium saucepan. Cook over medium heat until bubbly, stirring often. Cook 2 minutes more; remove from heat. Gradually stir half of hot mixture into egg yolks. Return to saucepan. Bring mixture to a boil over medium-high heat. Reduce heat to low and cook 2 minutes; remove from heat. Stir in yogurt, butter and almond extract.

3. To serve, spoon filling into bottoms of cream puffs. Pile orange sections on top of filling. Add cream puff tops. Lightly sift powdered sugar over tops.

Cream Puffs

> 1 **cup water**
> ½ **cup (1 stick) butter**
> 1 **cup all-purpose flour**
> ½ **teaspoon salt**
> 4 **eggs**

1. Preheat oven to 400°F. Grease baking sheet.

2. Combine water and butter in medium saucepan; bring to a boil, stirring until butter melts. Add flour and salt all at once, stirring vigorously. Cook and stir until mixture forms ball that does not separate. Remove from heat and cool 10 minutes. Add eggs, 1 at a time, beating after each addition until mixture is smooth.

3. Drop heaping tablespoonfuls of batter into 6 mounds, 3 inches apart, on prepared baking sheet. Bake about 35 minutes or until golden brown and puffy. Cool slightly. Cut off tops and remove soft dough inside. Cool completely on wire rack.

MAKES 6 SERVINGS

> **Cream Puffs (recipe follows)**
> ¾ **cup granulated sugar**
> 3 **tablespoons cornstarch**
> 1½ **cups orange juice**
> 3 **egg yolks, beaten**
> 1 **cup plain low-fat yogurt**
> 2 **tablespoons butter**
> ½ **teaspoon almond extract**
> 1 **can (11 ounces) mandarin oranges, drained**
> **Powdered sugar**

Muffins and Coffee Cakes

Breakfast breads take center stage in this tempting collection of recipes

Jalapeño Corn Muffins

1½ cups yellow cornmeal

¾ cup all-purpose flour

2 teaspoons baking powder

½ teaspoon baking soda

½ teaspoon salt

2 eggs

4 tablespoons butter, melted and cooled

2 tablespoons sugar

¾ cup buttermilk

1 can (8 ounces) cream-style corn

1 cup Monterey Jack or Cheddar cheese

2 fresh jalapeño peppers,* seeded and finely chopped

1. Preheat oven and greased muffin tin to 400°F. If using silicone muffin cups, lightly coat with nonstick cooking spray and place in hot oven 5 minutes before filling.

2. Place cornmeal, flour, baking powder, baking soda and salt in bowl of electric stand mixer. Mix at low speed until combined. In separate bowl, whisk eggs. Add butter and sugar; stir. Add buttermilk; mix gently.

3. Add egg mixture to flour mixture in bowl of electric stand mixer. Beat at medium speed until combined. Add corn, cheese and peppers to batter. Mix at low speed until combined; do not overbeat.

4. Fill muffin cups three-fourths full. Bake 15 to 17 minutes or until muffins are golden brown. Let cool 5 minutes before serving.

Jalapeño peppers can sting and irritate the skin, so wear rubber gloves when handling peppers and do not touch your eyes.

Cherry-Coconut-Cheese Coffee Cake

2½ cups all-purpose flour

¾ cup sugar

½ teaspoon baking powder

½ teaspoon baking soda

2 packages (3 ounces each) cream cheese, softened, divided

¾ cup milk

2 tablespoons vegetable oil

2 eggs

1 teaspoon vanilla

½ cup sweetened flaked coconut

¾ cup cherry preserves

2 tablespoons butter

1. Preheat oven to 350°F. Grease and flour 9-inch springform pan. Combine flour and sugar in large bowl. Reserve ½ cup flour mixture. Stir baking powder and baking soda into remaining flour mixture. Cut in 1 package cream cheese with pastry blender or 2 knives until mixture resembles coarse crumbs; set aside.

2. Combine milk, oil and 1 egg in medium bowl. Add to cream cheese mixture; stir just until moistened. Spread batter on bottom and 1 inch up side of prepared pan. Combine remaining package cream cheese, remaining egg and vanilla in small bowl; stir until smooth. Pour over batter, spreading to within 1 inch of edge. Sprinkle coconut over cream cheese mixture. Spoon preserves evenly over coconut.

3. Cut butter into reserved flour mixture with pastry blender or 2 knives until mixture resembles coarse crumbs. Sprinkle over preserves. Bake 55 to 60 minutes or until golden brown and toothpick inserted into crust comes out clean. Cool in pan on wire rack 15 minutes. Remove side of pan; serve warm.

Chocolate Chunk Coffee Cake

1¾ cups all-purpose flour

1 teaspoon baking powder

1 teaspoon baking soda

½ teaspoon salt

¾ cup packed brown sugar

½ cup (1 stick) butter, softened

3 eggs

1 teaspoon vanilla

1 cup sour cream

1 package (about 11 ounces) semisweet chocolate chunks

1 cup chopped nuts

1. Preheat oven to 350°F. Grease 13×9-inch baking pan.

2. Combine flour, baking powder, baking soda and salt in medium bowl. Place brown sugar and butter in bowl of electric stand mixer; beat at medium speed until creamy. Add eggs and vanilla; beat until well blended. Alternately add flour mixture and sour cream; beat until blended. Stir in chocolate chunks and nuts. Spread batter evenly into prepared pan.

3. Bake 25 to 35 minutes or until toothpick inserted into center comes out clean. Cool in pan on wire rack.

Lemon Poppy Seed Muffins

MAKES 18 MUFFINS

- 2 **cups all-purpose flour**
- 1¼ **cups granulated sugar**
- ¼ **cup poppy seeds**
- 2 **tablespoons plus 2 teaspoons grated lemon peel, divided**
- 2 **teaspoons baking powder**
- ½ **teaspoon baking soda**
- ½ **teaspoon ground cardamom**
- ¼ **teaspoon salt**
- 2 **eggs**
- ½ **cup (1 stick) butter, melted**
- ½ **cup milk**
- ½ **cup plus 2 tablespoons lemon juice, divided**
- 1 **cup powdered sugar**

1. Preheat oven to 400°F. Grease 18 standard (2½-inch) muffin cups or line with paper baking cups.

2. Combine flour, granulated sugar, poppy seeds, 2 tablespoons lemon peel, baking powder, baking soda, cardamom and salt in large bowl. Beat eggs in medium bowl. Add butter, milk and ½ cup lemon juice; mix well. Add egg mixture to flour mixture; stir just until blended. Spoon batter evenly into prepared muffin cups, filling three-fourths full.

3. Bake 15 to 20 minutes or until toothpick inserted into centers comes out clean. Cool in pans on wire racks 10 minutes.

4. Meanwhile, prepare glaze. Combine powdered sugar and remaining 2 teaspoons lemon peel in small bowl; stir in enough remaining lemon juice to make pourable glaze. Place muffins on sheet of foil or waxed paper; drizzle with glaze. Serve warm or at room temperature.

Citrus Butter

MAKES ABOUT 1 CUP

- 1 **cup butter, softened**
- ¾ **teaspoon grated orange peel**
- 2 **tablespoons fresh orange juice**
- ¼ **teaspoon lime peel**

1. Place butter, orange peel, orange juice and lime peel in bowl of electric stand mixer. Beat at medium speed until well blended.

2. Place butter mixture on sheet of waxed paper. Using waxed paper to hold butter mixture, roll it back and forth to form a log. Wrap log in plastic wrap.

3. Store in airtight container in refrigerator up to 2 weeks.

Serving Note: This butter makes a delicious complement to sweet muffins and scones.

Lemon Poppy Seed Muffins

Jumbo Streusel-Topped Raspberry Muffins

MAKES 6 JUMBO MUFFINS

2¼ cups all-purpose flour, divided

¼ cup packed brown sugar

2 tablespoons cold butter

¾ cup granulated sugar

2 teaspoons baking powder

½ teaspoon baking soda

½ teaspoon salt

½ teaspoon grated lemon peel

¾ cup plus 2 tablespoons milk

⅓ cup butter, melted

1 egg, beaten

2 cups fresh or frozen raspberries (do not thaw)

1. Preheat oven to 350°F. Grease 6 jumbo (3½-inch) muffin cups.

2. For streusel topping, combine ¼ cup flour and brown sugar in small bowl. Cut in cold butter with pastry blender or 2 knives until mixture forms coarse crumbs. Set aside.

3. Reserve ¼ cup flour in medium bowl. Place remaining 1¾ cups flour, granulated sugar, baking powder, baking soda, salt and lemon peel in bowl of electric stand mixer; mix at low speed 30 seconds. Combine milk, melted butter and egg in small bowl.

4. Add milk mixture to flour mixture; mix at low speed until almost blended. Toss raspberries with reserved flour just until coated; gently fold raspberries into muffin batter. Spoon batter into prepared muffin cups, filling three-fourths full. Sprinkle with streusel topping.

5. Bake 25 to 30 minutes or until toothpick inserted into centers comes out clean. Cool in pan 2 minutes; remove to wire rack. Serve warm or at room temperature.

Variation: For smaller muffins, spoon batter into 12 standard (2½-inch) greased or paper-lined muffin cups. Bake at 350°F for 21 to 24 minutes or until toothpick inserted into centers comes out clean. Makes 12 muffins.

Blueberry Poppy Seed Coffee Cake

1½ cups all-purpose flour

½ cup sugar

1 teaspoon baking powder

½ teaspoon baking soda

¼ teaspoon salt

¼ cup (½ stick) cold butter, cut into small pieces

1 tablespoon poppy seeds

¾ cup low-fat buttermilk

1 egg

1 teaspoon vanilla

1 teaspoon grated lemon peel

1 cup fresh blueberries

1. Preheat oven to 350°F. Spray 9-inch round cake pan with nonstick cooking spray; set aside.

2. Combine flour, sugar, baking powder, baking soda and salt in large bowl. Cut in butter using pastry blender or 2 knives until mixture resembles coarse crumbs. Stir in poppy seeds.

3. Whisk buttermilk, egg, vanilla and lemon peel in small bowl until blended. Stir buttermilk mixture into flour mixture just until flour mixture is moistened. Spread half of batter into prepared pan; top with blueberries. Drop remaining batter in 8 dollops onto blueberries, leaving some berries uncovered. Bake 33 to 36 minutes or until top is golden brown.

4. Cool 15 minutes in pan on wire rack. Serve warm.

Bacon-Cheddar Muffins

MAKES 12 MUFFINS

2 cups all-purpose flour

¾ cup sugar

2 teaspoons baking powder

½ teaspoon baking soda

½ teaspoon salt

¾ cup plus 2 tablespoons milk

⅓ cup butter, melted and cooled

1 egg

1 cup (4 ounces) shredded Cheddar cheese

6 slices bacon, crisp-cooked and crumbled

1. Preheat oven to 350°F. Grease 12 standard (2½-inch) muffin cups.

2. Place flour, sugar, baking powder, baking soda and salt in bowl of electric stand mixer. Mix at low speed 30 seconds or just until combined. Combine milk, butter and egg in small bowl; mix well. Add milk mixture to flour mixture; mix at low speed until blended. Add cheese and bacon; mix at low speed 30 seconds more. Spoon batter into prepared muffin cups, filling three-fourths full.

3. Bake 15 to 20 minutes or until toothpick inserted into centers comes out clean. Cool in pan 2 minutes; remove to wire rack. Serve warm or at room temperature.

Marmalade Muffins

MAKES 18 MUFFINS

2 cups all-purpose flour

2 teaspoons baking powder

¾ teaspoon salt

1 cup (2 sticks) unsalted butter, softened

1½ cups sugar

2 eggs

1½ teaspoons vanilla

1 cup orange marmalade, plus more for topping

1 cup buttermilk

1. Preheat oven to 350°F. Line muffin pan with paper baking cups.

2. In medium bowl, sift flour, baking powder and salt; set aside.

3. Beat butter and sugar in bowl of electric stand mixer at high speed until light and fluffy, about 5 minutes. Add eggs, 1 at a time, and beat until blended. Add vanilla; mix at low speed 30 seconds. Fold in half the dry mixture just until moistened. Mix in 1 cup marmalade and remaining dry mixture.

4. Stir in buttermilk; do not overmix. Fill baking cups three-fourths full. Bake 20 to 25 minutes or until edges are golden brown and toothpick inserted into centers comes out clean. Top with additional marmalade.

Boston Brown Bread Muffins

MAKES 12 MUFFINS

- ½ **cup rye flour**
- ½ **cup whole wheat flour**
- ½ **cup yellow cornmeal**
- ¾ **teaspoon salt**
- 1½ **teaspoons baking soda**
- 1 **egg**
- ⅓ **cup molasses**
- ⅓ **cup packed dark brown sugar**
- ⅓ **cup dark beer**
- 1 **cup buttermilk**
- 1 **cup golden raisins**
  Softened cream cheese

1. Preheat oven to 400°F. Grease 12 standard (2½-inch) muffins cups. Place flours, cornmeal, salt and baking soda in bowl of electric stand mixer. Mix at low speed 30 seconds or until combined. In another bowl, combine egg, molasses, brown sugar, beer and buttermilk. Add to flour mixture along with raisins; mix at low speed until combined.

2. Fill prepared muffin cups. Bake 15 minutes or until toothpick inserted into centers comes out clean. Serve with cream cheese.

Double Chocolate Zucchini Muffins

1. Preheat oven to 400°F. Line 12 (3½-inch) muffin cups with paper baking cups or spray with nonstick cooking spray.

2. Place flour, sugar, cocoa, baking powder, cinnamon, baking soda and salt in bowl of electric stand mixer. Mix at low speed 30 seconds. Combine sour cream, oil, eggs and milk in medium bowl until blended; add to flour mixture. Mix at low speed just until moistened. Fold in chocolate chips and zucchini. Spoon batter into prepared muffin cups, filling half full.

3. Bake 25 to 30 minutes or until toothpick inserted into centers comes out clean. Cool in pan on wire rack 5 minutes. Remove from pan. Cool completely on wire rack. Store tightly covered at room temperature.

Variation: For standard-size muffins, spoon batter into 18 standard (2½-inch) paper-lined or greased muffin cups. Bake at 400°F for 18 to 20 minutes or until toothpick inserted into centers comes out clean.

MAKES 12 JUMBO MUFFINS

- 2⅓ **cups all-purpose flour**
- 1¼ **cups sugar**
- ⅓ **cup unsweetened cocoa powder**
- 2 **teaspoons baking powder**
- 1½ **teaspoons ground cinnamon**
- 1 **teaspoon baking soda**
- ½ **teaspoon salt**
- 1 **cup sour cream**
- ½ **cup vegetable oil**
- 2 **eggs, beaten**
- ¼ **cup milk**
- 1 **cup milk chocolate chips**
- 1 **cup shredded zucchini**

Pumpkin Chocolate Chip Muffins

MAKES 18 MUFFINS

2½ cups all-purpose flour

1 tablespoon baking powder

1½ teaspoons pumpkin pie spice*

½ teaspoon salt

1 cup solid-pack pumpkin

1 cup packed light brown sugar

¾ cup milk

2 eggs

6 tablespoons butter, melted

1 cup semisweet chocolate chips

½ cup chopped walnuts

Or substitute ¾ teaspoon ground cinnamon, ⅜ teaspoon ground ginger, and scant ¼ teaspoon each ground allspice and ground nutmeg for 1½ teaspoons pumpkin pie spice.

1. Preheat oven to 400°F. Line 18 standard (2½-inch) muffin cups with paper baking cups or spray with nonstick cooking spray.

2. Combine flour, baking powder, pumpkin pie spice and salt in bowl of electric stand mixer. Beat pumpkin, brown sugar, milk, eggs and butter in medium bowl until well blended. Add pumpkin mixture, chocolate chips and walnuts to flour mixture; mix at low speed 30 seconds or just until moistened. Spoon evenly into prepared muffin cups, filling two-thirds fulll.

3. Bake 15 to 17 minutes or until toothpick inserted into centers comes out clean. Cool in pans on wire racks 10 minutes; remove from pans and cool completely on wire racks.

Easy Peach Streusel Coffee Cake

1. Preheat oven to 375°F. Spray 9-inch square baking pan with nonstick cooking spray.

2. For coffee cake, place 2 cups baking mix in medium bowl; break up lumps with spoon. Add milk, egg, granulated sugar, cinnamon and vanilla; stir until well blended. Add peaches; stir just until blended. Pour batter into prepared pan.

3. For topping, combine remaining ½ cup baking mix and brown sugar in small bowl; stir until well blended. Add pecans and butter; toss gently (do not break up small pieces of butter). Sprinkle evenly over batter.

4. Bake 35 minutes or until toothpick inserted into center comes out clean. Cool in pan on wire rack 15 minutes. Serve warm or at room temperature.

MAKES 9 SERVINGS

- 2½ **cups biscuit baking mix, divided**
- ⅔ **cup whole milk**
- 1 **egg**
- ¼ **cup granulated sugar**
- 1 **teaspoon ground cinnamon**
- 1 **teaspoon vanilla**
- 1 **pound frozen unsweetened peaches, thawed and diced**
- ½ **cup packed dark brown sugar**
- ½ **cup pecan pieces**
- 3 **tablespoons cold butter, diced**

Pepper Cheese Muffins

MAKES 24 MINIATURE MUFFINS

1 **cup buttermilk**

⅓ **cup butter, melted**

2 **eggs**

2 **cups all-purpose flour**

4 **ounces (1 cup) shredded pepper jack cheese**

1 **tablespoon sugar**

2 **teaspoons baking powder**

1 **teaspoon chopped fresh parsley**

½ **teaspoon baking soda**

¼ **teaspoon salt**

¼ **teaspoon coarsely ground black pepper**

1. Place buttermilk, butter and eggs in bowl of electric stand mixer. Attach flat beater to mixer. Turn to medium and beat 1 minute. Stop and scrape bowl. Combine flour, cheese, sugar, baking powder, parsley, baking soda, salt and pepper in medium bowl. Turn mixer to low and add flour mixture, mixing just until moistened, about 30 seconds. Do not overbeat.

2. Fill greased miniature muffin tins two-thirds full. Bake at 400°F for 15 to 20 minutes. Serve warm.

Raspberry Corn Muffins

1. Preheat oven to 350°F. Spray 12 standard (2½-inch) muffin cups with nonstick cooking spray.

2. Combine flour, cornmeal, baking powder, baking soda and salt in small bowl; set aside. Whisk together egg, sour cream and apple juice concentrate. Add flour mixture to egg mixture. Stir just until dry ingredients are moistened. Do not overmix. Gently stir in raspberries.

3. Spoon batter into prepared muffin cups, filling each cup three-fourths full. Bake 18 to 20 minutes or until golden brown. Let stand in pan on wire rack 5 minutes. Remove from pan; cool slightly.

4. Combine cream cheese and fruit spread in small serving bowl. Serve with warm muffins.

MAKES 12 MUFFINS

- 1 **cup all-purpose flour**
- ¾ **cup cornmeal**
- 2 **teaspoons baking powder**
- ½ **teaspoon baking soda**
- ¼ **teaspoon salt**
- 1 **egg, beaten**
- 1 **cup reduced-fat sour cream**
- ⅓ **cup thawed, frozen unsweetened apple juice concentrate**
- 1½ **cups fresh or frozen raspberries**
- ⅔ **cup reduced-fat whipped cream cheese**
- 2 **tablespoons raspberry fruit spread**

Raisin-Wheat Muffins

MAKES 18 MUFFINS

2 eggs

⅓ cup yogurt

⅔ cups warm milk
(105°F to 115°F)

⅓ cup honey

⅓ cup vegetable oil

2 cups whole wheat flour

¾ teaspoon salt

1 teaspoon baking soda

⅓ cup raisins

1. Place eggs in bowl of electric stand mixer. Attach wire whip to mixer. Turn to low and mix 15 seconds. Add yogurt and milk. Turn to medium and beat 15 seconds.

2. Add honey, oil, flour, salt, baking soda and raisins. Turn to low and mix until well blended, about 15 seconds.

3. Pour batter into ungreased muffin tins. Bake at 425°F for 15 minutes.

Apricot Butter

MAKES 16 SERVINGS

1 cup (5 ounces) dried apricots

1 cup unsweetened apple juice

1. Combine apricots and juice in small saucepan; bring to a boil over medium-high heat. Reduce heat to low; cover and simmer 20 minutes, stirring occasionally. Remove from heat; cool slightly.

2. Pour mixture into blender or food processor; process until smooth. Cool to room temperature and refrigerate in airtight container or jar with tight-fitting lid up to 3 months.

Serving Note: This "butter" is a delicious and healthy alternative topping for muffins, toast, biscuits or coffee cake.

Orange-Chocolate Chip Muffins

1. Preheat oven to 350°F. Spray 12 muffin cups with nonstick cooking spray or line with paper baking cups.

2. Combine flour, sugar, baking soda, baking powder and salt in large bowl. Mix milk, oil, eggs and orange peel in medium bowl until well blended. Add milk mixture and chocolate chips to flour mixture; stir just until moistened. Spoon evenly into prepared muffin cups, about ½ cup batter per cup.

3. Bake 25 to 28 minutes or until toothpick inserted into centers comes out clean. Cool muffins in pan on wire rack 5 minutes. Remove from pan; cool completely on wire rack.

MAKES 12 MUFFINS

3	cups all-purpose flour
1¼	cups sugar
1½	teaspoons baking soda
1	teaspoon baking powder
½	teaspoon salt
1¼	cups milk
¾	cup vegetable oil
2	eggs
	Grated peel of 1 orange (3 to 4 teaspoons)
1	cup semisweet chocolate chips

Spicy Sweet Potato Muffins

MAKES 12 MUFFINS

⅓ cup plus 2 tablespoons packed brown sugar, divided

2 teaspoons ground cinnamon, divided

1½ cups all-purpose flour

2 teaspoons baking powder

½ teaspoon salt

½ teaspoon baking soda

½ teaspoon ground allspice

1 cup cooked and mashed or canned sweet potatoes

¾ cup buttermilk

¼ cup vegetable oil

1 egg, beaten

1. Preheat oven to 425°F. Grease 12 standard (2½-inch) muffin cups.

2. Combine 2 tablespoons brown sugar and 1 teaspoon cinnamon in small bowl; set aside.

3. Sift flour, baking powder, remaining 1 teaspoon cinnamon, salt, baking soda and allspice into large bowl. Stir in remaining ⅓ cup brown sugar.

4. Combine sweet potatoes, buttermilk, oil and egg in medium bowl. Stir buttermilk mixture into dry ingredients just until moistened. Spoon batter into prepared muffin cups, filling each two-thirds full. Sprinkle each muffin with ½ teaspoon cinnamon mixture. Bake 14 to 16 minutes or until toothpick inserted into centers comes out clean.

Honey Butter

MAKES ABOUT ¾ CUP

½ cup (1 stick) butter, softened

⅓ cup honey

1 teaspoon grated orange peel

1. Place butter in bowl of electric stand mixer. Beat at medium speed until fluffy. Add honey; beat until well blended. Add orange peel; mix at low speed until blended.

2. Place butter mixture on sheet of waxed paper. Using waxed paper to hold butter mixture, roll it back and forth to form a log. Wrap log in plastic wrap.

3. Store in airtight container in refrigerator up to 2 weeks.

Chocolate-Pecan Coffee Cake

1. Preheat oven to 350°F. Spray 13×9-inch baking pan with nonstick cooking spray.

2. Combine chocolate chunks, pecans, ¾ cup sugar and cinnamon in medium bowl. Combine flour, baking soda, baking powder and salt in separate medium bowl.

3. Place butter, remaining 1¼ cups sugar and vanilla in bowl of electric stand mixer; beat at medium speed until light and fluffy. Add eggs, 1 at a time, beating well after each addition. Add flour mixture alternately with sour cream, beating well after each addition. Spread half of batter into prepared pan; sprinkle with half of chocolate chunk mixture. Top with remaining batter and chocolate chunk mixture.

4. Bake about 40 minutes or until toothpick inserted into center comes out clean. Cool in pan on wire rack.

MAKES 15 SERVINGS

1 **package (12 ounces) semisweet chocolate chunks or chips**

1 **cup chopped pecans**

2 **cups sugar, divided**

1 **teaspoon ground cinnamon**

2¾ **cups all-purpose flour**

1½ **teaspoons baking soda**

1 **teaspoon baking powder**

¾ **teaspoon salt**

¾ **cup (1½ sticks) butter, softened**

1 **teaspoon vanilla**

3 **eggs**

1½ **cups sour cream**

Pies, Tarts, and Cobblers

Buttery pastry plus decadent filling equals a delicious slice of comfort

Chocolate Pecan Pie

MAKES 1 PIE

4 **eggs**

1 **cup sugar**

1 **cup dark corn syrup**

3 **(1-ounce) squares unsweetened chocolate, melted**

2 **cups pecan halves**

1 **(9-inch) Perfect Pie Pastry shell, unbaked (see recipe on page 194)**

1. Beat eggs, sugar and corn syrup in bowl of electric stand mixer at medium-high speed 1 minute. Stop and scrape bowl.

2. Turn mixer to medium speed and gradually add in chocolate; beat 1 minute or until well blended. Stir in pecans. Pour mixture into pastry shell. Bake at 350°F for 35 to 45 minutes or until slightly soft in center.

Strawberry Cream Pie

MAKES 8 SERVINGS

1 cup plus 1½ teaspoons all-purpose flour, divided

¼ cup plus 1 teaspoon sugar, divided

¼ teaspoon salt

¼ cup cold butter, cut into pieces

3 tablespoons ice water, divided

¾ teaspoon white or cider vinegar

6 ounces fat-free cream cheese

2 ounces Neufchâtel cheese

¼ cup vanilla fat-free yogurt

2 egg whites

½ teaspoon vanilla

1½ cups fresh strawberries, cut in half

¼ cup strawberry jelly

1. Combine 1 cup flour, 1 teaspoon sugar and salt in medium bowl. Cut in butter using 2 knives or pastry blender until mixture resembles coarse crumbs. Add 2 tablespoons ice water and vinegar; stir until moist but slightly firm dough forms. If necessary, add remaining 1 tablespoon ice water. Form dough into ball.

2. Preheat oven to 450°F. Roll out dough into 12-inch circle on lightly floured surface. Place dough in 9-inch glass pie dish. Bake 10 to 12 minutes or until lightly browned. Cool on wire rack. Reduce oven temperature to 325°F.

3. Place cream cheese, Neufchâtel cheese, remaining ¼ cup sugar and remaining 1½ teaspoons flour in bowl of electric stand mixer. Beat at medium speed until creamy. Beat in yogurt, egg whites and vanilla; mix well. Pour cream cheese mixture into pie crust. Bake 25 minutes or until set. Cool completely on wire rack.

4. Place strawberries on top of filling. For glaze, melt jelly over low heat in small saucepan. Carefully brush glaze over strawberries, allowing glaze to run onto cheese mixture. Refrigerate 3 hours or overnight. Cut into 8 wedges.

Perfect Pie Pastry

MAKES 2 (8- OR 9-INCH) CRUSTS

2¼ **cups all-purpose flour**

¾ **teaspoon salt**

½ **cup shortening, well chilled**

2 **tablespoons butter, well chilled**

5 **to 6 tablespoons cold water**

1. Place flour and salt in bowl of electric stand mixer. Turn to low and mix 15 seconds. Cut shortening and butter into pieces and add to flour mixture. Turn to low and mix until shortening particles are size of small peas, 30 to 45 seconds.

2. Continuing at low speed, add water, 1 tablespoon at a time, mixing until ingredients are moistened and dough begins to hold together. Divide dough in half. Pat each half into smooth ball and flatten slightly. Wrap in plastic wrap. Chill in refrigerator 15 minutes.

3. Roll half of dough to ⅛-inch thickness between waxed paper. Fold pastry into quarters. Ease into 8- or 9-inch pie plate and unfold, pressing firmly against bottom and sides.

For One-Crust Pie: Fold edge under. Crimp as desired. Add desired pie filling. Bake as directed.

For Two-Crust Pie: Trim pastry even with edge of pie plate. Using second half of dough, roll out another pastry crust. Add desired pie filling. Top with second pastry crust. Seal edge. Crimp as desired. Cut slits for steam to escape. Bake as directed.

For Baked Pastry Shell: Fold edge under. Crimp as desired. Prick sides and bottom with fork. Bake at 450°F for 8 to 10 minutes or until lightly browned. Cool completely on wire rack and fill.

Alternate Method for Baked Pastry Shell: Fold edge under. Crimp as desired. Line shell with foil. Fill with pie weights or dried beans. Bake at 450°F for 10 to 12 minutes or until edges are lightly browned. Remove pie weights and foil. Cool completely on wire rack and fill.

Classic Country Apple Pie

1. Combine sugar, flour, cinnamon, nutmeg and salt in large bowl. Stir in apples.

2. Fill Perfect Pie Pastry shell with apple mixture and dot with butter. Sprinkle top crust with sugar, if desired.

3. Bake at 400°F for 50 minutes.

MAKES 8 SERVINGS

- 1 **cup sugar, plus additional for topping (optional)**
- 2 **tablespoons all-purpose flour**
- 1 **teaspoon ground cinnamon**
- ⅛ **teaspoon ground nutmeg**
- ⅛ **teaspoon salt**
- 6 **to 8 medium tart cooking apples, peeled, cored and thinly sliced**
- 1 **Perfect Pie Pastry shell, unbaked (see recipe on page 194)**
- 2 **tablespoons butter, cut into pieces**

Boston Cream Pie

MAKES 1 (9-INCH) PIE

1 cup granulated sugar

⅓ cup shortening

1 egg

1 teaspoon vanilla

1¼ cups all-purpose flour

1½ teaspoons baking powder

½ teaspoon salt

¾ cup milk

Cream Filling (recipe follows)

Chocolate Glaze (recipe follows)

1. Preheat oven to 350°F. Grease and flour 9-inch round cake pan. Place granulated sugar and shortening in bowl of electric stand mixer. Mix at medium-low speed until light and fluffy. Add egg and vanilla; mix at low speed until combined. Combine flour, baking powder and salt in small bowl. Add flour mixture to sugar mixture alternately with milk, beating well after each addition. Pour into prepared pan. Bake 35 minutes or until toothpick inserted in center comes out clean. Cool in pan 10 minutes.

2. Meanwhile, prepare Cream Filling. Loosen edge of cake and remove to rack to cool completely. Prepare Chocolate Glaze. When cake is cool, split in half horizontally to make 2 thin layers. To assemble, spoon Cream Filling over bottom half of cake; cover with top half. Spread top with Chocolate Glaze; cool. Serve when glaze is completely set. Refrigerate.

Cream Filling: Combine ⅓ cup granulated sugar, 2 tablespoons cornstarch and ¼ teaspoon salt in 2-quart saucepan. Gradually stir in 1½ cups milk. Cook over medium heat, stirring constantly, until mixture thickens and comes to a boil. Boil 1 minute, stirring constantly. Gradually stir small amount of hot mixture into 2 slightly beaten egg yolks; mix thoroughly. Return to hot mixture in pan. Bring to a boil; boil 1 minute, stirring constantly. Do not overcook. Remove from heat; stir in 2 teaspoons vanilla. Cool to room temperature. Chill.

Chocolate Glaze: Combine 2 (1-ounce) squares unsweetened chocolate and 3 tablespoons butter in medium saucepan; cook and stir over low heat until melted. Remove from heat; stir in 1 cup sifted powdered sugar and 1 teaspoon vanilla. Stir in 3 to 5 teaspoons water, 1 teaspoon at a time, until glaze is of desired consistency. Cool slightly.

Pumpkin Ice Cream Pie with Caramel Sauce

MAKES 8 SERVINGS

25 **gingersnap cookies, finely crushed (about 1½ cups)**

¼ **cup (½ stick) butter, melted**

2 **tablespoons granulated sugar**

4 **cups pumpkin ice cream, softened (about 1 quart)**

1 **cup packed dark brown sugar**

½ **cup whipping cream**

6 **tablespoons (¾ stick) unsalted butter**

¼ **cup light corn syrup**

½ **teaspoon salt**

1 **cup pecan halves, toasted**

To toast pecans, spread them on baking sheet and place in preheated 350°F oven 8 to 10 minutes.

1. Coat 9-inch pie plate with nonstick cooking spray. Preheat oven to 350°F.

2. For crust, combine cookie crumbs, melted butter and granulated sugar in medium bowl; mix well. Press onto bottom and side of prepared pie plate. Bake 8 minutes. Cool completely on wire rack.

3. Fill crust with ice cream; smooth top. Cover and freeze 1 hour.

4. For sauce, whisk brown sugar, cream, unsalted butter, corn syrup and salt in medium saucepan over medium-high heat until sugar dissolves and mixture comes to a boil. Reduce heat; boil 1 minute without stirring. Remove from heat and cool.

5. Cut pie into wedges; top with caramel sauce and toasted pecans.

Oats 'n' Apple Tart

MAKES 8 SERVINGS

1½ cups quick oats

½ cup packed brown sugar, divided

1 tablespoon plus ¼ teaspoon ground cinnamon, divided

5 tablespoons butter, melted

2 medium sweet apples, such as Golden Delicious, unpeeled, cored and thinly sliced

1 teaspoon lemon juice

¼ cup water

1 envelope unflavored gelatin

½ cup apple juice concentrate

1 package (8 ounces) reduced-fat cream cheese, softened

⅛ teaspoon ground nutmeg

1. Preheat oven to 350°F. Combine oats, ¼ cup brown sugar and 1 tablespoon cinnamon in medium bowl. Add butter and stir until combined. Press into bottom and up side of 9-inch pie plate. Bake 7 minutes or until set. Cool on wire rack.

2. Toss apple slices with lemon juice in small bowl; set aside. Place water in small saucepan. Sprinkle gelatin over water; let stand 3 to 5 minutes. Stir in apple juice concentrate. Cook and stir over medium heat until gelatin is dissolved. Do not boil. Remove from heat and set aside.

3. Beat cream cheese in bowl of electric stand mixer at medium speed until fluffy and smooth. Add remaining ¼ cup brown sugar, ¼ teaspoon cinnamon and nutmeg. Mix until smooth. Slowly add gelatin mixture at low speed until blended and creamy, about 1 minute. Do not overmix.

4. Arrange apple slices in crust. Pour cream cheese mixture evenly over top. Refrigerate 2 hours or until set.

Lemon Curd Tart with Fresh Blueberries

MAKES 6 SERVINGS

4 **sheets phyllo dough
   (12×17 inches)**

⅔ **cup butter, melted**

   **Lemon Curd Filling
   (recipe follows)**

½ **pint fresh blueberries**

1. Place 1 sheet phyllo dough on clean work surface. Keep remaining phyllo sheets under damp cloth until ready to use. Brush surface of sheet with butter. Place another sheet on top and brush with butter. Repeat with remaining dough sheets and butter.

2. Cut dough into 6 equal squares. Fit 1 square into each cup of well-greased muffin tin. Pleat dough to fit, if necessary. Work quickly so dough does not dry out. Bake at 375°F for 12 to 14 minutes.

3. To serve, place one sixth of Lemon Curd Filling (about ⅓ cup) into each tart shell. Sprinkle each with fresh blueberries. Serve immediately.

Lemon Curd Filling

¾ **cup sugar**

½ **cup plus 1 tablespoon lemon juice**

6 **large egg yolks**

½ **cup (1 stick) butter, at room temperature**

1. Place sugar and lemon juice in bowl of electric stand mixer. Attach wire whip to mixer. Turn to medium-low and mix 1 minute.

2. Increase to medium and add egg yolks, one at a time, whipping about 30 seconds after each addition. Continuing at medium speed, add butter, 1 tablespoon at a time, mixing about 15 seconds after each addition. Whip an additional 30 seconds. Mixture will appear curdled.

3. Transfer mixture to medium saucepan. Cook over medium-low heat, stirring constantly, until mixture is thick and smooth and just begins to bubble, about 7 to 8 minutes. Do not allow mixture to boil.

4. Pour filling into medium bowl and press plastic wrap onto surface of lemon curd. Refrigerate until cold, at least 4 hours.

Mascarpone Cheese Tart with Candied Almonds

MAKES 12 SERVINGS

Crust

- ¼ **cup slivered almonds**
- ¾ **cup graham cracker crumbs**
- 3 **tablespoons melted butter**
- 1½ **tablespoons sugar**

Filling

- 4 **ounces cream cheese, softened**
- ¼ **cup sugar**
- 2 **eggs**
- ½ **teaspoon vanilla**
- 16 **ounces mascarpone cheese**

Topping

- ¾ **cup strawberry preserves**
- **Candied Almonds (recipe follows, optional)**

1. Preheat oven to 375°F. Place 9-inch tart pan with removable bottom on baking sheet.

2. For Crust, place slivered almonds in food storage bag; seal and crush using rolling pin. Combine almonds, graham cracker crumbs, butter and sugar in small bowl; mix well. Press into bottom and up sides of tart pan. Bake 10 minutes or until golden and set. Cool completely.

3. Reduce oven temperature to 325°F. For Filling, beat cream cheese in bowl of electric stand mixer at medium speed 1 minute or until smooth. Beat in sugar. Add eggs, 1 at a time, then vanilla, beating well after each addition. Add mascarpone; beat at high speed about 20 seconds or until smooth. Do not overmix.

4. Spread Filling in Crust; bake 60 to 80 minutes or until golden and puffed. (Filling will settle as tart cools.) Cool completely.

5. For Topping, melt strawberry preserves in small saucepan over low heat. Spread over tart. Refrigerate until cold. To serve, remove tart from pan and garnish with candied almonds, if desired.

Candied Almonds

- 3 **tablespoons plus 2 teaspoons sugar**
- 3 **tablespoons water**
- 1⅓ **cups whole almonds**
- **Butter-flavored cooking spray**

1. Cook sugar and water in medium saucepan over medium-low heat until candy thermometer registers 230°F. Remove from heat. Add almonds and let sit about 2 minutes or until sugar is sandy. Return pan to low heat. Cook, stirring constantly, until sugar melts and caramelizes on almonds.

2. Transfer almonds to nonstick baking sheet; spray with butter-flavored cooking spray. Break almonds apart with spatula. Cool 3 minutes, then use hands to separate almonds, if necessary.

Pear and Cranberry Cobbler

MAKES 6 TO 8 SERVINGS

Biscuit Topping

- 1 **cup all-purpose flour**
- 2 **tablespoons sugar**
- 2 **teaspoons baking powder**
- ¼ **teaspoon salt**
- ¼ **cup (½ stick) cold butter, cubed**
- ½ **cup milk**

Filling

- 4 **cups diced peeled ripe pears (3 to 4 medium pears)**
- 2 **cups fresh cranberries**
- ½ **cup sugar**
- 3 **tablespoons all-purpose flour**
- ¼ **teaspoon ground cinnamon**
- 2 **tablespoons butter, cut into pieces**

1. Preheat oven to 375°F. Lightly grease 10-inch round or oval baking dish.

2. For Biscuit Topping, combine 1 cup flour, 2 tablespoons sugar, baking powder and salt in medium bowl. Cut in butter with pastry blender or 2 knives until mixture forms coarse crumbs. Stir in milk until soft, sticky dough forms; set aside.

3. For Filling, combine pears, cranberries, ½ cup sugar, 3 tablespoons flour and cinnamon; stir gently. Spoon into prepared baking dish. Dot with butter. Drop Biscuit Topping by tablespoonfuls onto Filling.

4. Place baking dish on baking sheet; bake 25 to 35 minutes or until topping is golden and filling is bubbly. Serve warm.

Chocolate Walnut Toffee Tart

MAKES 12 SERVINGS

  2 **cups all-purpose flour**

1½ **cups plus 3 tablespoons sugar, divided**

  ¾ **cup (1½ sticks) cold butter, cut into pieces**

  2 **egg yolks**

1¼ **cups whipping cream**

  1 **teaspoon ground cinnamon**

  2 **teaspoons vanilla**

1¼ **cups semisweet chocolate chunks or chips, divided**

  2 **cups coarsely chopped walnuts**

1. For crust, preheat oven to 325°F. Place flour and 3 tablespoons sugar in food processor; pulse just until mixed. Scatter butter pieces over flour mixture; process 20 seconds. Add egg yolks; process 10 seconds (mixture may be crumbly).

2. Transfer dough to ungreased 10-inch tart pan with removable bottom or 9- to 10-inch pie pan. Press dough firmly and evenly into pan. Bake 10 minutes or until surface is no longer shiny.

3. Increase oven temperature to 375°F. Combine cream, remaining 1½ cups sugar and cinnamon in large saucepan; bring to a boil over medium-high heat. Reduce heat to low; simmer 10 minutes, stirring frequently. Remove pan from heat and stir in vanilla.

4. Sprinkle 1 cup chocolate chunks and walnuts evenly over partially-baked crust. Pour cream mixture over top. Bake 35 to 40 minutes or until tart is bubbling and lightly browned. Cool completely in pan on wire rack.

5. Place remaining ¼ cup chocolate chunks in small resealable food storage bag. Microwave on HIGH 20 seconds; knead bag until chocolate is melted. Cut small hole in 1 corner of bag; drizzle chocolate over tart.

Note: Tart may be made up to 5 days in advance. Cover with plastic wrap and refrigerate until ready to serve.

Lemon Cheesecake Tarts

MAKES 4 DOZEN TARTS

1 recipe Basic Shortbread
   Dough (see recipe on
   page 22)
2 teaspoons grated lemon peel

Filling

1 package (8 ounces) cream
   cheese, softened
¼ cup sugar
½ cup prepared lemon curd
   Lemon peel (optional)
   Fresh mint (optional)

1. Prepare Basic Shortbread Dough, adding lemon peel to butter and sugar mixture. Divide dough into 2 discs. Wrap each disc in plastic wrap. Refrigerate at least 1 hour or until firm.

2. Remove dough from refrigerator; let stand 5 minutes. Lightly spray 48 mini (1¾-inch) muffin cups with nonstick cooking spray.

3. On lightly floured surface, roll out 1 dough disc to ⅛ inch thick. Cut out circles with 2½-inch round or fluted cookie cutter. Place circles in muffin cups, pressing dough down against bottom and sides. Press together any cracks. Repeat with second dough disc. Re-roll dough scraps once. Refrigerate mini tarts at least 30 minutes.

4. Preheat oven to 375°F. Prick holes in bottom of each tart using fork tines. Bake 10 to 12 minutes or until golden brown. Cool completely in pans on wire rack before removing from muffin cups.

5. For Filling, beat cream cheese and sugar in bowl of electric stand mixer at medium-low speed 2 minutes. Add lemon curd; stir until combined. Fill tart shells with about 2 teaspoons Filling.

6. Cover and refrigerate at least 2 hours and up to 3 days before serving. Garnish with lemon peel and mint. Store covered in refrigerator.

Berry-Peachy Cobbler

MAKES 8 SERVINGS

- 4 tablespoons plus 2 teaspoons sugar, divided
- ¾ cup plus 2 tablespoons all-purpose flour
- 1¼ pounds peaches, peeled and sliced or 1 package (16 ounces) frozen unsweetened sliced peaches, thawed and drained
- 2 cups fresh raspberries or 1 package (12 ounces) frozen unsweetened raspberries
- 1 teaspoon grated lemon peel
- ½ teaspoon baking powder
- ½ teaspoon baking soda
- ⅛ teaspoon salt
- 2 tablespoons cold butter, cut into small pieces
- ½ cup low-fat buttermilk

1. Preheat oven to 425°F. Spray 8 ramekins with nonstick cooking spray; place ramekins on jellyroll pan. Set aside.

2. For filling, combine 2 tablespoons sugar and 2 tablespoons flour in large bowl. Add peaches, raspberries and lemon peel; toss to coat. Divide fruit among prepared ramekins. Bake about 15 minutes or until fruit is bubbly around edges.

3. Meanwhile, for topping, combine remaining ¾ cup flour, 2 tablespoons sugar, baking powder, baking soda and salt in medium bowl. Cut in butter using pastry blender or 2 knives until mixture resembles coarse crumbs. Stir in buttermilk just until dry ingredients are moistened.

4. Remove ramekins from oven; top fruit with equal dollops of topping. Sprinkle topping with remaining 2 teaspoons sugar. Bake 18 to 20 minutes or until topping is lightly browned. Serve warm.

Fabulous Fruit Tart

MAKES 8 SERVINGS

- 1 **Perfect Pie Pastry shell, unbaked (see recipe on page 194)**
- 1 **package (8 ounces) reduced-fat cream cheese, softened**
- ⅓ **cup no-sugar-added raspberry fruit spread**
- ½ **cup sliced peaches or nectarines***
- ⅓ **cup sliced strawberries***
- ½ **cup kiwifruit slices***
- ⅓ **cup raspberries***
- 3 **tablespoons no-sugar-added apricot pourable fruit****
- 2 **teaspoons raspberry-flavored liqueur (optional)**

*Sliced bananas, plums, or blueberries can be substituted.

**Or substitute 2 tablespoons no-sugar-added apricot fruit spread combined with 1 tablespoon warm water.

1. Preheat oven to 350°F. Roll out pastry to 12-inch circle; place in 10-inch tart pan with removable bottom or 10-inch quiche dish. Prick bottom and sides of pastry with fork. Bake 18 to 20 minutes or until golden brown. Cool completely on wire rack.

2. Combine cream cheese and fruit spread; mix well. Spread onto bottom of cooled pastry. Chill at least 1 hour.

3. Just before serving, arrange fruit over cream cheese layer. Combine pourable fruit and liqueur, if desired; brush evenly over fruit.

Onion, Cheese and Tomato Tart

MAKES 6 TO 8 SERVINGS

Parmesan-Pepper Dough
(recipe follows)
1 tablespoon butter
1 medium onion, thinly sliced
1 cup (4 ounces) shredded
Swiss cheese
2 to 3 ripe tomatoes, sliced
Black pepper
2 tablespoons chopped fresh
chives

1. Prepare Parmesan-Pepper Dough.

2. Melt butter in large skillet over medium heat. Add onion; cook and stir 20 minutes or until tender.

3. Spread onion over prepared dough. Sprinkle with cheese. Let rise in warm place 20 to 30 minutes or until edges are puffy.

4. Preheat oven to 400°F. Top cheese with tomatoes. Sprinkle with pepper. Bake 25 minutes or until edges are deep golden and cheese is melted. Let cool 10 minutes. Transfer to serving platter. Sprinkle with chives.

Parmesan-Pepper Dough

1 package (¼ ounce) active dry yeast
1 tablespoon sugar
⅔ cup warm water (105°F to 115°F)
2 cups all-purpose flour, divided
¼ cup grated Parmesan cheese
1 teaspoon salt
½ teaspoon black pepper
1 tablespoon olive oil

1. Sprinkle yeast and sugar over warm water in small bowl; stir until yeast is dissolved. Let stand 5 minutes or until mixture is bubbly.

2. Place 1¾ cups flour, cheese, salt and pepper in bowl of electric stand mixer; mix at low speed 1 minute or just until combined. Pour yeast mixture and oil over flour mixture; mix at medium-low until mixture clings together.

3. Attach dough hook to mixer. Knead 2 to 3 minutes at low speed or until dough is smooth and elastic, adding remaining ¼ cup flour if necessary. Shape dough into ball; place in large greased bowl, turning to grease top. Cover. Let rise in warm place 1 hour or until doubled in bulk.

4. Punch down dough; turn out onto lightly floured surface. Knead 1 minute or until smooth. Flatten into disc. Roll dough to make 11-inch round. Press into bottom and up sides of buttered 9- or 10-inch tart pan with removable bottom.

Deep-Dish Streusel Peach Pie

MAKES ABOUT 6 SERVINGS

- 1 can (29 ounces) or 2 cans (16 ounces each) cling peach slices in syrup
- 1/3 cup plus 1 tablespoon granulated sugar, divided
- 1 tablespoon cornstarch
- 1/2 teaspoon vanilla
- 1/2 cup packed brown sugar
- 2 cups all-purpose flour, divided
- 1/3 cup quick oats
- 1/4 cup (1/2 stick) butter, melted
- 1/2 teaspoon ground cinnamon
- 1/2 teaspoon salt
- 1/2 cup shortening
- 4 to 5 tablespoons cold water
- Sweetened Whipped Cream (recipe follows)

1. Drain peach slices, reserving 3/4 cup syrup. Combine 1/3 cup granulated sugar and cornstarch in small saucepan. Gradually add reserved syrup; stir until well blended. Cook and stir over low heat until thickened. Remove from heat; stir in vanilla. Set aside.

2. Combine brown sugar, 1/2 cup flour, oats, butter and cinnamon in small bowl; stir until mixture forms coarse crumbs. Set aside.

3. Preheat oven to 350°F. Combine remaining 1 1/2 cups flour, remaining 1 tablespoon granulated sugar and salt in small bowl. Cut in shortening until mixture resembles coarse meal. Sprinkle water, 1 tablespoon at a time, over flour mixture. Toss lightly with fork until mixture holds together. Press together to form ball. Press dough between hands to form 5- to 6-inch disc. Roll dough into 1/8-inch-thick square on lightly floured surface. Cut into 10-inch square. Press dough into bottom and 1 inch up sides of 8-inch square baking dish. Arrange peaches over crust. Pour sauce over peaches. Sprinkle with crumb topping. Bake 45 minutes.

4. Prepare Sweetened Whipped Cream. Serve warm or at room temperature with Sweetened Whipped Cream.

Sweetened Whipped Cream

- 1 cup whipping cream, chilled
- 3 tablespoons sugar
- 1/2 teaspoon vanilla

Chill bowl and wire whip attachment of electric stand mixer. Pour chilled whipping cream into bowl and beat at high speed until soft peaks form. Gradually add sugar and vanilla. Whip until stiff peaks form.

Italian Chocolate Pie

1. Toast pine nuts in dry nonstick skillet over medium heat, stirring constantly until golden brown and aromatic. Remove from heat. Finely chop; cool. Combine pine nuts, brown sugar and orange peel in small bowl. Sprinkle onto bottom of pie crust; gently press into crust.

2. Preheat oven to 325°F. Melt chocolate and butter in small saucepan over low heat; stir until blended and smooth. Let cool to room temperature.

3. Place chocolate mixture and evaporated milk in bowl of electric stand mixer. Beat at medium speed 2 minutes or until combined. Add eggs, 1 at a time, beating well after each addition. Stir in hazelnut liqueur and vanilla. Pour into pie crust.

4. Bake on center rack of oven 30 to 40 minutes or until filling is set.

5. Cool completely on wire rack. Refrigerate until ready to serve. Serve with whipped cream and chocolate curls.

MAKES 8 SERVINGS

- ¼ cup pine nuts
- 3 tablespoons packed brown sugar
- 1 tablespoon grated orange peel
- 1 Perfect Pie Pastry shell, unbaked (see recipe on page 194)
- 4 ounces bittersweet chocolate, coarsely chopped
- 3 tablespoons unsalted butter
- 1 can (5 ounces) evaporated milk
- 3 eggs
- 3 tablespoons hazelnut liqueur
- 1 teaspoon vanilla
  Whipped cream (optional)
  Chocolate curls (optional)

Scones and Biscuits

Sweet and savory quick breads perfect for breakfast or a midday snack

Parmesan Peppercorn Biscuits

2 cups all-purpose flour

1 tablespoon baking powder

½ teaspoon salt

1 teaspoon freshly ground black pepper

⅓ cup finely grated Parmesan cheese

6 tablespoons (¾ stick) butter, chilled

1 cup buttermilk

1. Preheat oven to 425°F. Combine flour, baking powder, salt, pepper and Parmesan in large mixing bowl. Using pastry blender or 2 knives, cut in butter until mixture resembles coarse crumbs.

2. Add buttermilk; stir just until ingredients are moist and well combined.

3. Drop ¼-cup mounds of dough onto parchment-lined baking sheet. Bake 12 to 15 minutes or until tops of biscuits are golden brown. Remove from oven; let sit 3 to 5 minutes before serving.

Coconut Scones with Orange Butter

MAKES 8 SCONES

1¾ **cups all-purpose flour**

½ **teaspoon salt**

1 **tablespoon baking powder**

2 **tablespoons sugar**

5 **tablespoons butter**

1 **egg**

1 **cup cream, divided**

2 **tablespoons milk**

2 **teaspoons grated orange peel**

½ **cup plus ⅓ cup sweetened flaked coconut, divided**

Orange Butter (recipe follows)

1. Preheat oven to 400°F. Combine flour, salt, baking powder and sugar in large mixing bowl. Using pastry blender or 2 knives, cut butter into dry ingredients until mixture resembles coarse meal; set aside.

2. Place egg, ¾ cup cream, milk, orange peel and ½ cup coconut in separate mixing bowl. Mix until just combined. Add egg mixture to flour mixture. Stir quickly until dough forms.

3. Transfer dough to lightly floured surface. Pat into 8-inch circle, about ¾ inch thick. Cut into 8 equal triangles. Brush tops of scones with remaining ¼ cup cream; sprinkle with remaining ⅓ cup coconut.

4. Place scones 2 inches apart on parchment-lined baking sheet. Bake 12 to 15 minutes or until scones are golden brown and coconut is toasted. Cool on wire rack 15 minutes. Halve and serve with Orange Butter.

Orange Butter

½ **cup butter, softened**

2 **tablespoons freshly squeezed orange juice**

1 **tablespoon grated orange peel**

2 **teaspoons sugar**

Place all ingredients in bowl of electric stand mixer. Mix at low speed until creamy and well blended.

Makes about 1 cup

Honey Scones with Cherry Compote

2 cups all-purpose flour

½ teaspoon salt

1 tablespoon baking powder

2 tablespoons packed brown sugar

1 tablespoon granulated sugar

½ cup old-fashioned oats

6 tablespoons butter, melted and cooled

1 large egg

3 tablespoons honey

¼ cup heavy cream

¼ cup milk

Butter

Cherry Compote (recipe follows)

1. Preheat oven to 400°F. Whisk together flour, salt, baking powder, sugars and oatmeal in large mixing bowl; set aside. Whisk together butter, egg, honey, cream and milk in separate bowl. Add butter mixture to flour mixture. Stir quickly until dough forms.

2. Transfer dough to lightly floured surface. Pat dough into 8-inch round, about ¾ inch thick. Cut into 8 triangles. Place scones 1 to 2 inches apart on parchment-lined baking sheet.

3. Bake 12 to 15 minutes or until scones are golden brown. Cool on wire racks 15 minutes. Halve and serve with butter and Cherry Compote.

Cherry Compote

1 pound fresh Bing cherries, pitted and halved

¼ cup sugar

¼ cup water

2 tablespoons freshly squeezed lemon juice

1. Combine all ingredients in heavy-bottomed saucepan. Cook over medium heat until sugar is dissolved and liquid is boiling. Boil 2 minutes and remove cherries with slotted spoon; set aside.

2. Reduce heat to medium-low; simmer liquid 2 to 4 minutes or until mixture thickens.

3. Return cherries to pan and remove from heat. Cool 1 hour before serving.

Makes about 2 cups

Mustard Beer Biscuits

MAKES 12 BISCUITS

- 2 cups all-purpose flour
- 2 teaspoons baking powder
- ¾ teaspoon salt
- ¼ cup cold shortening
- ¼ cup cold butter
- ½ cup beer
- 1 tablespoon plus 1 teaspoon prepared mustard, divided
- 1 tablespoon milk

tip

Consider serving these biscuits alongside a hearty bowl of chili, or halve them and top with cold cuts, sharp Cheddar cheese, and additional mustard for an extra-special sandwich.

1. Preheat oven to 425°F. In large bowl, combine flour, baking powder and salt. Cut in shortening and butter until mixture resembles coarse crumbs. Combine beer and 1 tablespoon mustard in separate small bowl. Stir beer mixture into crumb mixture. Mix just until combined. Turn dough onto floured surface; knead gently 8 times.

2. Pat dough to ½-inch thickness. Cut out biscuits with 2-inch round biscuit cutter. Reroll scraps and cut out additional biscuits. Place biscuits 1 inch apart on greased baking sheet. Combine remaining mustard with milk and brush over tops. Bake 13 to 15 minutes or until lightly browned.

Cranberry & White Chocolate Scones

MAKES 8 SCONES

- 1 cup all-purpose flour
- 1 cup whole wheat flour
- ¼ cup plus 1 tablespoon sugar, divided
- 2 teaspoons baking powder
- ½ teaspoon salt
- ½ teaspoon ground nutmeg
- 6 tablespoons cold butter, cut into ½-inch pieces
- 1 cup dried cranberries
- 1 cup white chocolate chips
- 2 eggs
- ⅓ cup plus 1 tablespoon whipping cream, divided
- Grated peel of 1 orange (3 to 4 teaspoons)

1. Preheat oven to 425°F. Line baking sheet with parchment paper. Combine all-purpose flour, whole wheat flour, ¼ cup sugar, baking powder, salt and nutmeg in large bowl. Cut in butter with pastry blender or 2 knives until mixture resembles coarse crumbs. Stir in cranberries and white chips.

2. Beat eggs in small bowl; whisk in ⅓ cup cream and orange peel. Make well in flour mixture; add egg mixture and stir with fork just until mixture forms dough. Knead dough 8 to 10 times on lightly floured surface.

3. Shape dough into disc; place on prepared baking sheet and press into 9-inch circle. Score dough into 8 wedges with sharp knife. Brush with remaining 1 tablespoon cream; sprinkle with remaining 1 tablespoon sugar.

4. Bake 20 to 23 minutes or until edges are lightly browned and toothpick inserted into center comes out clean. Remove to cutting board; cut into wedges along score lines. Cool completely on wire rack.

Cheddar & Onion Drop Biscuits

MAKES 12 BISCUITS

3¾ cups Better Baking Mix
    (recipe follows)

¼ cup canola oil

1¼ cups cold fat-free (skim) milk,
    low-fat buttermilk or soy milk

¼ cup shredded low-fat
    Cheddar cheese

¼ cup sliced green onions

1. Preheat oven to 400°F.

2. Place Better Baking Mix in large mixing bowl. Cut in oil with pastry blender or 2 knives until mixture resembles coarse meal. Make well in center of mixture and add milk. Gently stir mixture together just until moistened. Do not overmix. Gently fold in cheese and onions with rubber spatula.

3. Using ¼-cup measure or 2-inch ice cream scoop, scoop 12 pieces of dough onto baking sheet, placing 1 inch apart. (Dipping cup or scoop in water between scoops helps batter release easier onto baking sheet.)

4. Bake 10 to 12 minutes, rotating pan once during baking, until biscuits are golden brown on tops and bottoms and toothpick inserted in center comes out clean. Remove from oven; serve immediately or transfer to wire rack to cool.

Better Baking Mix

2¼ cups unbleached all-purpose flour

2¼ cups whole wheat flour

2¼ cups oat flour*

1¼ cups nonfat dry milk

3 tablespoons baking powder

1½ teaspoons salt

1 teaspoon baking soda

Oat flour is available at many supermarkets, natural foods stores, and online. Oat flour can easily be made at home by pulsing old-fashioned oats in blender or food processor until flour-like consistency is reached.

1. Combine ingredients in 1-gallon resealable freezer food storage bag; stir with wire whisk to blend. Seal bag; shake upside down to mix ingredients in corners.

2. Alternatively, combine ingredients in large bowl; transfer to 8-cup container with tight-fitting lid; seal. Label and date. Store in freezer up to 6 months.

Note: Freezing is suggested for Better Baking Mix because whole wheat and oat flours are made with whole grains, meaning they still contain the bran, germ and endosperm of the grain. Whole grains contain more beneficial fats and fiber than refined grains, and should be frozen for longer shelf life.

Makes 8 cups

Cranberry-Orange Scones

½ **cup dried cranberries**

1 **cup hot water**

3¾ **cups Better Baking Mix (see recipe on page 230)**

¼ **cup sugar**

¼ **cup butter**

1¼ **cups cold fat-free (skim) milk**

1 **tablespoon grated orange peel**

Ground cinnamon (optional)

tip

Use the thin, bright orange part of orange skin for grated orange peel. Avoid using any bitter white pith. You can use a simple tool called a zester or a small, sharp paring knife to peel the orange and then mince it.

1. Preheat oven to 400°F. Lightly spray baking sheet with nonstick cooking spray; set aside.

2. Soak cranberries in hot water about 10 minutes or until softened; drain.

3. Meanwhile, combine Better Baking Mix and sugar in large bowl. Cut in butter with pastry blender or 2 knives until mixture resembles coarse crumbs. Make well in center of mixture and add milk. Gently stir together just until mixed. Do not overmix. Gently fold in drained cranberries and orange peel.

4. Scoop 12 pieces of dough 1 inch apart onto baking sheet, using ¼-cup measure or 2-inch ice cream scoop. (Dipping cup or scoop in water between scoops helps batter release easier onto baking sheet.) Sprinkle lightly with cinnamon, if desired.

5. Bake 10 to 12 minutes, rotating baking sheet once during baking, or until scones are golden brown on tops and toothpick inserted into centers comes out clean. Serve immediately or cool on wire rack.

Lemon-Cardamom Scones with Lemon Drizzle

MAKES 8 SCONES

1¼ cups all-purpose flour

¾ cup oat bran

2 tablespoons granulated sugar

2 teaspoons grated lemon peel, divided

2 teaspoons baking powder

¾ teaspoon ground cardamom

¼ teaspoon baking soda

¼ teaspoon salt

¼ cup (½ stick) cold butter

1 egg, lightly beaten

1 container (6 ounces) low-fat lemon yogurt

3 tablespoons powdered sugar

2 teaspoons lemon juice

1. Preheat oven to 400°F. Lightly coat baking sheet with nonstick cooking spray; set aside.

2. Combine flour, oat bran, granulated sugar, 1½ teaspoons lemon peel, baking powder, cardamom, baking soda and salt in large bowl. Cut in butter with pastry blender or 2 knives until mixture resembles coarse meal.

3. Stir together egg and yogurt in small bowl until blended. Stir egg mixture into flour mixture just until moistened. On lightly floured surface gently knead dough 10 to 12 times. Pat dough into 7½-inch circle. Cut into 8 wedges. Place wedges 2 inches apart on prepared baking sheet.

4. Bake 11 to 13 minutes or until scones are golden brown. Remove from baking sheet to wire rack. Cool 10 minutes. Stir together powdered sugar, lemon juice and remaining ½ teaspoon lemon peel until smooth; drizzle over scones.

Lemon-Ginger Scones: Substitute ground ginger for ground cardamom.

Mustard-Pepper Biscuits

MAKES 14 BISCUITS

2 cups all-purpose flour

1 tablespoon baking powder

1 teaspoon sugar

¾ teaspoon black pepper

½ teaspoon salt

⅛ teaspoon garlic powder

3 tablespoons cold butter

¾ cup fat-free (skim) milk

2 tablespoons Dijon mustard

1. Preheat oven to 450°F. Lightly spray large baking sheet with nonstick cooking spray.

2. Combine flour, baking powder, sugar, pepper, salt and garlic powder in medium bowl. Cut in butter with pastry blender or 2 knives until mixture resembles coarse crumbs.

3. Whisk together milk and mustard in small bowl. Add to flour mixture. Stir just until dry ingredients are moistened. Drop dough by rounded tablespoonfuls 1 inch apart on prepared baking sheet. Bake about 10 minutes or until golden brown. Remove from pan to wire rack.

Baking Powder Biscuits

MAKES 12 BISCUITS

2 cups all-purpose flour

4 teaspoons baking powder

½ teaspoon salt

⅓ cup shortening

⅔ cup low-fat (1%) milk

Melted butter, if desired

1. Place flour, baking powder, salt and shortening in bowl of electric stand mixer. Turn to low and mix about 1 minute. Stop and scrape bowl.

2. Continuing on low, add milk and mix until dough starts to cling to beater. Do not overbeat. Turn dough onto lightly floured surface and knead about 20 seconds or until smooth. Pat or roll to ½-inch thickness. Cut with floured 2-inch biscuit cutter.

3. Place on greased baking sheets and brush with melted butter, if desired. Bake at 450°F for 12 to 15 minutes. Serve immediately.

Confetti Scones

MAKES 24 SCONES

2 teaspoons olive oil

⅓ cup minced red bell pepper

⅓ cup minced green bell pepper

½ teaspoon dried thyme

1 cup all-purpose flour

¼ cup whole wheat flour

1½ teaspoons baking powder

½ teaspoon baking soda

½ teaspoon sugar

¼ teaspoon ground red pepper

⅛ teaspoon salt

⅓ cup sour cream

⅓ cup fat-free (skim) milk

2 tablespoons minced green onions

¼ cup grated Parmesan cheese

Nonstick cooking spray

1. Preheat oven to 400°F. Line baking sheet with parchment paper; set aside.

2. Heat oil in small skillet over medium heat. Add bell peppers and thyme; cook and stir 5 minutes or until tender. Set aside. Combine flours, baking powder, baking soda, sugar, red pepper and salt in large bowl. Add sour cream, milk and green onions. Mix to form sticky dough. Stir in cheese. (Do not overmix.)

3. Drop dough by rounded tablespoonfuls onto prepared baking sheet. Spray tops lightly with cooking spray. Place in oven and immediately reduce heat to 375°F. Bake 13 to 15 minutes or until golden brown.

Ham & Swiss Cheese Biscuits

- 2 cups all-purpose flour
- 2 teaspoons baking powder
- ½ teaspoon baking soda
- ½ cup (1 stick) butter, chilled and cut into pieces
- ½ cup (2 ounces) shredded Swiss cheese
- 2 ounces ham, minced
- ⅔ cup buttermilk

1. Preheat oven to 450°F. Grease baking sheet.

2. Sift flour, baking powder and baking soda into medium bowl. Cut in butter with pastry blender or 2 knives until mixture resembles coarse crumbs. Stir in cheese, ham and enough buttermilk to make soft dough.

3. Turn out dough onto lightly floured surface; knead lightly. Roll out dough ½ inch thick. Cut out biscuits with 2-inch round cutter. Place on prepared baking sheet.

4. Bake about 10 minutes or until golden brown.

Cherry Scones

1. Preheat oven to 425°F. In large bowl, combine flours, sugar, baking powder and salt. Cut in shortening with pastry blender or 2 knives until mixture resembles coarse crumbs. Combine egg, beer and milk in separate small bowl; stir into crumb mixture. Stir in cherries. Turn onto floured surface; knead gently 4 times.

2. Shape dough into ball and place on ungreased baking sheet. Pat into 8-inch circle. Score dough into 8 wedges (do not separate). Sprinkle with raw sugar. Bake 18 to 22 minutes or until golden brown. Cut into wedges. Serve with fruit and preserves, if desired.

MAKES 8 SCONES

- 1½ cups all-purpose flour
- 1 cup whole wheat flour
- 3 tablespoons granulated sugar
- 2 teaspoons baking powder
- ¼ teaspoon salt
- ½ cup butter-flavored shortening
- 1 egg, beaten
- ½ cup honey beer
- ⅓ cup milk
- ¾ cup dried cherries
- 1 teaspoon raw sugar
- Fresh fruit (optional)
- Cherry preserves (optional)

Pumpkin-Ginger Scones

½ **cup sugar, divided**

2 **cups all-purpose flour**

2 **teaspoons baking powder**

1 **teaspoon ground cinnamon**

½ **teaspoon baking soda**

½ **teaspoon salt**

4 **tablespoons cold butter**

1 **egg**

½ **cup solid-pack pumpkin**

¼ **cup sour cream**

½ **teaspoon grated fresh ginger or 2 tablespoons finely chopped crystallized ginger**

1 **tablespoon butter, melted**

1. Preheat oven to 425°F.

2. Reserve 1 tablespoon sugar. Combine remaining sugar, flour, baking powder, cinnamon, baking soda and salt in large bowl. Cut in cold butter with pastry blender or 2 knives until mixture resembles coarse crumbs. Beat egg at medium-low speed in bowl of electric stand mixer. Add pumpkin, sour cream and ginger; beat on medium-low until well blended. Stir pumpkin mixture into flour mixture until it forms a soft dough that leaves side of bowl.

3. Turn dough out onto well-floured surface. Knead 10 times. Roll dough using floured rolling pin into 9×6-inch rectangle. Cut into 6 (3-inch) squares. Cut each square diagonally in half, making 12 triangles; place scones 2 inches apart on ungreased baking sheets. Brush tops of triangles with melted butter and sprinkle with reserved sugar.

4. Bake 10 to 12 minutes or until golden brown. Cool 10 minutes on wire racks. Serve warm.

Chocolate Chip Scones

1. Preheat oven to 350°F. Lightly grease 2 cookie sheets. Combine flour, chocolate chips, raisins, sugar, baking powder, baking soda, salt and cinnamon in large bowl; mix until well combined.

2. Cut in butter with pastry blender or 2 knives until mixture resembles coarse crumbs. Beat buttermilk, 1 egg and vanilla in small bowl. Add to flour mixture; mix just until sticky dough is formed.

3. Using 2 tablespoons dough for each scone, drop dough onto prepared cookie sheets. Blend remaining egg and milk in small bowl; brush mixture over tops of scones.

4. Bake 12 to 14 minutes or until toothpick inserted into centers comes out clean. Cool 5 minutes on wire rack. Serve warm.

MAKES 24 SCONES

- 2 cups all-purpose flour
- 1 cup mini chocolate chips
- ¾ cup golden raisins
- ½ cup sugar
- 2 teaspoons baking powder
- ¼ teaspoon baking soda
- ¼ teaspoon salt
- ¼ teaspoon ground cinnamon
- ½ cup (1 stick) butter, cut into small pieces
- ½ cup buttermilk
- 2 eggs, divided
- ½ teaspoon vanilla
- 1 tablespoon milk

Peach-Almond Scones

2 cups all-purpose flour

¼ cup plus 1 tablespoon sugar, divided

2 teaspoons baking powder

½ teaspoon salt

5 tablespoons cold butter

½ cup sliced almonds, lightly toasted, divided

1 egg

2 tablespoons low-fat (1%) milk

1 can (16 ounces) peach halves or slices in juice, drained and finely chopped

½ teaspoon almond extract

1. Preheat oven to 425°F. Combine flour, ¼ cup sugar, baking powder and salt in large bowl. Cut in butter with pastry blender or 2 knives until mixture resembles coarse crumbs. Stir in ¼ cup almonds. Lightly beat egg and milk in small bowl. Reserve 2 tablespoons egg mixture. Stir peaches and almond extract into remaining egg mixture. Add peach mixture to flour mixture; stir until soft dough forms.

2. Place dough onto well-floured surface. Gently knead 10 to 12 times. Roll dough into 9×6-inch rectangle. Cut into 6 (3-inch) squares using floured knife. Cut diagonally into halves, making 12 triangles; place scones 2 inches apart on ungreased baking sheets. Brush triangles with reserved egg mixture. Sprinkle with remaining ¼ cup almonds and 1 tablespoon sugar.

3. Bake 10 to 12 minutes or until golden brown. Remove from baking sheets and cool on wire racks 10 minutes. Serve warm.

Cinnamon-Date Scones

1. Preheat oven to 425°F. Combine 2 tablespoons sugar and cinnamon in small bowl; set aside. Combine flour, remaining 2 tablespoons sugar, baking powder and salt in medium bowl. Cut in butter with pastry blender or 2 knives until mixture resembles coarse crumbs. Stir in dates; set aside.

2. Beat eggs in small bowl with fork. Add half-and-half; beat until well blended. Reserve 1 tablespoon egg mixture. Stir remaining egg mixture into flour mixture until soft dough clings together and forms ball.

3. Turn out dough onto well-floured surface. Knead gently 10 to 12 times. Roll dough into 9×6-inch rectangle. Cut rectangle into 6 (3-inch) squares. Cut each square diagonally in half. Place triangles 2 inches apart on ungreased baking sheets. Brush with reserved egg mixture; sprinkle with reserved cinnamon-sugar mixture. Bake 10 to 12 minutes or until golden brown. Immediately remove from baking sheets; cool on wire racks 10 minutes. Serve warm.

MAKES 12 SCONES

- 4 **tablespoons sugar, divided**
- ¼ **teaspoon ground cinnamon**
- 2 **cups all-purpose flour**
- 2½ **teaspoons baking powder**
- ½ **teaspoon salt**
- 5 **tablespoons cold butter**
- ½ **cup chopped pitted dates**
- 2 **eggs**
- ⅓ **cup half-and-half or milk**

Simply Scones

MAKES 16 SCONES

2 cups all-purpose flour
2 tablespoons sugar
2 teaspoons baking powder
½ teaspoon salt
⅓ cup butter, softened
2 eggs
½ cup heavy cream
1 teaspoon water

tip

Add flavor to simple scones with ingredients such as dried fruits, nuts, and bits of chocolate.

1. Place flour, sugar, baking powder, salt and butter in bowl of electric stand mixer. Attach flat beater to mixer. Turn to low and mix 30 seconds or until well blended. Stop and scrape bowl.

2. Add 1 egg and cream. Turn to low and mix 30 seconds or until soft dough forms. Knead dough 3 times on lightly floured surface. Divide dough in half. Pat each half into circle about ½ inch thick. Cut each circle into 8 wedges.

3. Place wedges 2 inches apart on greased baking sheets. Beat remaining egg and water together. Brush egg mixture over each wedge. Bake at 425°F for 10 to 12 minutes. Serve immediately.

Index

Index

Frostings

Index

Index

Scones

Tarts

Metric Conversion Chart

VOLUME MEASUREMENTS (dry)

¹/₈ teaspoon = 0.5 mL
¹/₄ teaspoon = 1 mL
¹/₂ teaspoon = 2 mL
³/₄ teaspoon = 4 mL
1 teaspoon = 5 mL
1 tablespoon = 15 mL
2 tablespoons = 30 mL
¹/₄ cup = 60 mL
¹/₃ cup = 75 mL
¹/₂ cup = 125 mL
²/₃ cup = 150 mL
³/₄ cup = 175 mL
1 cup = 250 mL
2 cups = 1 pint = 500 mL
3 cups = 750 mL
4 cups = 1 quart = 1 L

VOLUME MEASUREMENTS (fluid)

1 fluid ounce (2 tablespoons) = 30 mL
4 fluid ounces (¹/₂ cup) = 125 mL
8 fluid ounces (1 cup) = 250 mL
12 fluid ounces (1¹/₂ cups) = 375 mL
16 fluid ounces (2 cups) = 500 mL

WEIGHTS (mass)

¹/₂ ounce = 15 g
1 ounce = 30 g
3 ounces = 90 g
4 ounces = 120 g
8 ounces = 225 g
10 ounces = 285 g
12 ounces = 360 g
16 ounces = 1 pound = 450 g

DIMENSIONS

¹/₁₆ inch = 2 mm
¹/₈ inch = 3 mm
¹/₄ inch = 6 mm
¹/₂ inch = 1.5 cm
³/₄ inch = 2 cm
1 inch = 2.5 cm

OVEN TEMPERATURES

250°F = 120°C
275°F = 140°C
300°F = 150°C
325°F = 160°C
350°F = 180°C
375°F = 190°C
400°F = 200°C
425°F = 220°C
450°F = 230°C

BAKING PAN SIZES

Utensil	Size in Inches/Quarts	Metric Volume	Size in Centimeters
Baking or Cake Pan (square or rectangular)	8×8×2	2 L	20×20×5
	9×9×2	2.5 L	23×23×5
	12×8×2	3 L	30×20×5
	13×9×2	3.5 L	33×23×5
Loaf Pan	8×4×3	1.5 L	20×10×7
	9×5×3	2 L	23×13×7
Round Layer Cake Pan	8×1½	1.2 L	20×4
	9×1½	1.5 L	23×4
Pie Plate	8×1¼	750 mL	20×3
	9×1¼	1 L	23×3
Baking Dish or Casserole	1 quart	1 L	—
	1½ quarts	1.5 L	—
	2 quarts	2 L	—